Unreal Engine 5 Collision Essentials

Understanding Unreal Engine's Collision Framework

STEPHEN ULIBARRI

This book is dedicated to my amazing student base. My motivation stems from seeing the growth and success of my students, and if you succeed, I have succeeded.

Table of Contents

INTRODUCTION

My motivations for writing this book were two-fold. The first was to help my students understand the collision framework of Unreal Engine. Over the years, students have presented their frustrations—either in the forums, the Druid Mechanics Discord Community, or to me directly—in desperate search of guidance. These frustrations arise from game behavior differing drastically from expectations. In other words, bugs. They're frustrated about bugs.

Over time, I've seen a trend. Bugs that often frustrate or confuse developers the most are collision related. The player's weapon is clearly overlapping with an enemy—why aren't blood particles spawning? Why isn't the enemy taking any damage? The enemy's attacks use the same code—why can the enemy damage the player just fine? A single trigger volume in the level works like a charm, but after adding twelve, the frame rate tanks to 14 FPS. What's going on?

Sometimes a developer knows why their mechanics aren't working the way they want, but a clear-cut design decision isn't obvious. What is the best practice? What is the solution that will scale with the game project?

Much of this confusion stems from a lack of understanding of the collision framework in Unreal Engine. One of the disadvantages of such a versatile system is that there are so many choices, options, and freedoms. My goal for this book is to demystify the various points of confusion I see at the heart of the bugs that stump developers so often.

My second motivation for writing this book was a selfish one. I wrote this book for me. I wanted to clear up the points of confusion *I* had about Unreal Engine's collision framework. I wanted a handbook I could refer to when determining the proper solution for handling collision interactions. I wanted to clarify the points that confused me about the Unreal Engine collision framework. Do I understand it correctly? Am I using it properly? Are my collision queries doing what I intend and only what I intend? Are there overlaps or hit callbacks being triggered behind my back? Is there even a modicum of performance I can squeeze out of my systems, and are they robust? Will they break at scale?

Throughout my years of game development, both solo and as a member of various professional teams, I've observed and used many different conventions and protocols. Some of these I agreed with, and some I did not. While some problems have multiple valid solutions, some have unequivocally wrong ones. The only way to know the difference is to understand the systems being used.

Mistakes stem from various causes. Confusion regarding the systems being used is perhaps one of the most significant and can manifest as the most subtle and evasive bugs to detect.

It is my aim to clarify with this book the various concepts in the Unreal Engine collision framework, point out common misconceptions, and elucidate the proper use of the key components therein. It is my goal that by doing so, you will gain a better understanding of how Unreal Engine collision works, eliminate, and prevent bugs, and improve the performance of your game projects. I also aim to achieve these same goals for myself in the process.

1 - COLLISION FUNDAMENTALS

This is what happens when an unstoppable force meets an immovable object.

-The Joker, to Batman

To make sure we are on the same page, I believe it is important to establish some fundamental concepts that all developers, from programmers to content creators, should be familiar with.

While some of the properties and structure of the collision framework require a peek into C++ code, you don't have to know the C++ programming language to read and understand this book. What's important is that you gain an understanding of how the collision framework works and how to use it effectively. This you can achieve from this book, whether you program in C++, script in Blueprint, or create content in the Unreal Editor.

Collision Data

Unreal Engine Levels are populated with objects derived from the Actor class. Each Actor in a Level has at least one component—the Root Component. In fact, this is a member variable on the AActor class called RootComponent, of type USceneComponent (in UE5, this C++ variable is wrapped in a

TObjectPtr, but you get the idea). This is the component that defines the transform of the Actor. Every time you access an Actor's location via GetActorLocation() in C++ or **Get Actor Location** in Blueprint, you're retrieving the world-space location of the Actor's Root Component.

So, by default, this Root Component is just a plain old Scene Component. Objects of the Scene Component class are basic, as far as components go. You can't see them, as they have no visual representation. And, perhaps more notably, they have no collision.

It's not until we get to the Primitive Component class that we get collision on our components. UPrimitiveComponent, a direct child of the USceneComponent class, introduces collision. Every time you select a component in the **Components** panel of your Actor Blueprint and scroll down to the **Collision** section, you're looking at properties inherited from UPrimitiveComponent.

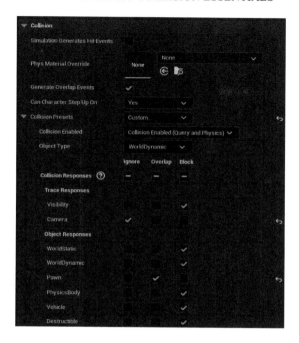

Figure 1.1 – Collision Settings in the Details Panel

Well, to be technical, many of these properties exist on a struct called BodyInstance, a member variable of type FBodyInstance on the Primitive Component class. These inner properties are exposed to the Details panel because BodyInstance is marked with a clever little UPROPERTY meta specifier that exposes inner properties: ShowOnlyInnerProperties. The BodyInstance variable contains some of the collision settings, such as the Collision Enabled and collision Object Type properties, which we'll discuss in more detail soon. Some of the collision settings are embedded further in an object of type UBodySetup within the Body Instance, but it doesn't really matter. The most important thing to understand here is that all these collision properties didn't exist in the Scene Component class—it's the Primitive Component class that introduces them, and the Primitive Component class that contains user-facing functions for changing them, and the Primitive Component class that is responsible for exposing them to the Details panel in Blueprint.

It is not the goal of this book to dive into the low-level machinations of Unreal Engine's C++ code, and for those who are not proficient in the C++ programming language, you don't need to know how to code to understand how the collision system works. It's enough to understand that collision stems from the Primitive Component, and it is via this class that we can access and modify a component's collision data.

So, what exactly do we mean by collision data?

Collision data consists of:

- Collision Geometry
- Collision Settings

Let's discuss.

Collision Geometry

It should make sense to you that geometry is required to have collision. A Scene Component has no collision because it does not contain the ability to store geometry information. As we've seen, a component must be derived from the Primitive

Component class to have collision.

Collision geometry can exist in various forms, depending on the type of component in question.

A Static Mesh has mesh geometry in the form of a triangle mesh. Though the triangle mesh is rarely used for collision, it can be. If a mesh did not contain simple collision when it was imported into an Unreal Engine project, a collision hull can be added from within the Static Mesh editor.

Collision Complexity

A Static Mesh asset will use either its simple or complex collision depending on its Collision Complexity property, accessible in the Details panel within the Static Mesh editor.

Figure 1.2 – Collision Complexity in the Static Mesh Editor

There are four choices:

- Project Default

- Simple and Complex

- Use Simple Collision as Complex

- Use Complex Collision as Simple

We'll analyze each one now.

Project Default

This is the default setting, which is determined by DefaultShapeComplexity in **Project Settings**. If you search for DefaultShapeComplexity in **Project Settings**, as of UE5.4, its default value will be Simple and Complex. This is because Simple and Complex is the most common choice.

Simple And Complex

Queries and collision tests use simple collision shapes because, as you may have guessed, simpler shapes make for simpler math, which is less computationally expensive. The "And Complex" part of Simple And Complex affects complex *queries*. Some utilities for performing queries allow the option to query the complex collision, which, as you should expect, is more expensive and done less often.

Use Simple Collision As Complex

You can ensure that only simple collision is used for all queries and collision tests by setting Collision Complexity to Use Simple Collision as Complex.

Use Complex Collision As Simple

You can also go the other way—only use the complex collision (the triangle mesh) by setting Collision Complexity to Use Complex Collision as Simple. If you do this, your mesh can only be static (it can't move). Think twice before using this setting. Collision hulls exist for a reason—to lighten the load on your hardware and improve the performance of your game. Opting to use complex geometry isn't a decision that should be made lightly.

It's worth noting that meshes created in Modeling Mode have this setting for their Collision Complexity by default. Adding a collision hull in the Static Mesh editor and changing the mesh's Collision Complexity right away is a good habit.

Collision Presets

Primitive Components have Collision Presets (a collision setting that we'll discuss in detail soon). Static Mesh assets also have their own Collision Presets, which can be seen and edited from within the Static Mesh editor.

The Shape Component class inherits collision settings from its parent, the Primitive Component. Shape Components are the collision volumes you typically add to actors to achieve some sort of overlap effect (though they're certainly not limited to that). Box Components, Sphere Components, the Capsule Component on the Character class are all examples of Shape Components.

Skeletal Mesh assets don't use collision hulls, but rather rely on Physics Assets. Physics Assets contain simple shapes of their own (called Physics Bodies), typically corresponding to bones on the Skeleton, allowing them to move along with the Skeletal Mesh while animating or simulating physics (such as when rag-dolling).

This isn't an exhaustive list, as there are other entities that can have collision, from landscapes to foliage. The important thing to understand is that geometry forms a crucial component to collision data, as geometry is what determines whether one object collides with another.

Queries

The word *query* literally means "question." And in game development, that's precisely what a query is. When you perform a query, you're asking the question "would I overlap or hit something if I were to do X?" Here, X can be:

- Performing a ray cast – shooting an imaginary line out into space and seeing what lies in its way.

- Performing a shape sweep – pushing an imaginary shape, be it a box, sphere, capsule, etc., out into the world and seeing what it hits/overlaps with.

- Performing an overlap test – checking to see if any components are overlapping with a component or specified shape.

In our games, we have "physical" objects (let's not get into a philosophical argument about whether or not meshes are actually physical, alright?) and some of them are moving. Because games are chaotic, intense, fun, and player controlled and/or AI-controlled, these objects are liable to get in each other's way. This may result in collision interactions between these physical objects. When we speak of queries, we are not speaking of these physical objects, but rather *hypothetical* objects. What would be the point of impact *if I were* to shoot an invisible sphere out into the world and hit an object?

Collision Callbacks

There are callbacks that are fired in response to objects moving into each other. These callbacks depend on the nature of the interaction, i.e. hit callbacks fire in response to blocking interactions, and overlap callbacks fire in response to overlapping interactions, etc. Example implementations of these callbacks include Blueprint events or C++ functions bound to the **On Component Begin Overlap** and **On Component Hit** delegates on the Primitive Component class. We'll discuss these in detail later on.

Collision Settings

One of the biggest sources of confusion in the Unreal Engine collision framework is collision settings. This is one of the easiest things to get wrong and is often the root of many collision-related bugs. If you take anything away from this book, it should be how to properly configure collision settings.

It's not enough for a component to have collision geometry. We must explicitly state how that geometry should behave. Games are an intertwining system of geometries that clash, overlap, and smash each other to bits, and what happens when two objects collide is determined by those objects' collision settings. It's our responsibility to determine exactly how an object should interact with other objects in its environment.

In the Collision section in the Details panel for any Primitive Component, there is a dropdown labeled Collision Presets. Depending on how long you've been developing games in Unreal Engine, this little dropdown just might be the bane of your existence.

Figure 1.3 – Collision Presets

The dropdown has some built-in choices. In the above figure, it's set to Custom... which is the only choice that allows you to override the settings revealed when you expand the presets with the triangle on the left in Figure 1.3.

The dropdown can also be set to Default for Static Meshes, which causes the inner settings to disappear entirely. This sets the component to use the default collision settings in the Static Mesh asset.

The rest of the choices are Collision Presets that are built into the engine. You can create your own custom presets, and we'll get into that later, but in a fresh project, these are all built-in presets. They are immutable, meaning that if you select a given preset, the collision settings therein are grayed out and cannot be changed. This is a strength, as opposed to a weakness, as we'll soon see.

Each time you open the Collision Presets for a given component, frustrated because your game isn't working properly, and set Collision Presets to Custom... you get an icky feeling in your stomach, and you should. That's because Custom... is not a well-defined preset, but more of a wildcard. If a component has its Collision Presets set to Custom..., it does not necessarily have the same collision settings as another component with its Collision Presets set to Custom..., in fact, it likely doesn't. And when things aren't working, it's difficult to know which of the many settings that you've tweaked is incorrect. When a component is using a collision preset, it has the same exact collision settings as all other components that use that collision preset. This makes it much easier to debug when a setting is incorrect, and once fixed, it's fixed for all components that use that preset. The habit of setting Collision Presets to Custom... on all of your components with collision is a habit that you're soon going to break, and more importantly, you'll understand why you should break it.

It's now time to dive deeper into collision settings.

2 - COLLISION PRESETS

Any component with collision has a set of properties that fully describe its collision interactions with other objects and queries. This set of properties comprises the component's collision profile.

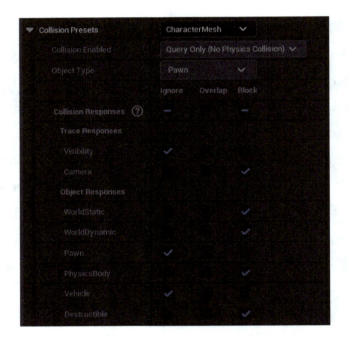

Figure 2.1 – The CharacterMesh Collision Profile

Collision Profile

A collision profile consists of three parts:

- A Collision Enabled **setting**

- **A collision** Object Type

- A set of Collision Responses

Collision Enabled

Collision Enabled is an enum which determines the type of collision for the component. Choices are:

- No Collision

- Query Only (No Physics Collision)

- Physics Only (No Query Collision)

- Collision Enabled (Query and Physics)

- Probe Only (Contact Data, No Query or Physics Collision)

- Query and Probe (Query Collision and Contact Data, No Physics Collision)

When setting Collision Enabled, ask yourself what this component will be doing in the game. If the component belongs to an Actor that already has another component (sphere, capsule, box, etc.) designated to handle collision, consider setting it to No Collision. Easy-peasy.

But we know it's not always that simple, don't we?

Let's discuss the different options and what they mean.

No Collision

This is the simplest of the options, and the most self-explanatory. The component will not have collision interactions with any other components or queries, no matter what those other objects or queries are using for their collision settings. If another component begins to occupy the same space as this component's geometry, it will pass straight through. If a query is performed, it will not detect this component. This is the most performant of the options since no calculations are necessary to detect any collisions with this component.

Query Only (No Physics Collision)

This setting designates the component for use only by spatial queries. Overlaps, line traces and shape sweeps will be able to detect this component, however this component will not be used for physics simulations. An object simulating physics, for example, will not bounce off this component, as physics collision is disabled for this component. This affords us some performance gains by avoiding physics computation.

Physics Only (No Query Collision)

This setting allows the component to participate in physics simulations, but not queries. The comment for this enum constant in C++ states "Useful for jiggly bits that do not need per bone detection." While this isn't the only use case, it's a pretty good comment, as it gives you an example for its use. We get performance gains for avoiding the need to detect queries.

Collision Enabled (Query and Physics)

The most expensive of the options thus far, this option gives us both queries and physics interactions. The default Capsule Component on the Character class uses this setting. A component using this setting will generate collision interactions with both spatial queries and physics bodies. Just hover a ball Static Mesh Actor over the third-person template Character with physics and gravity enabled. If collision filtering is set up properly (something we'll discuss soon), you should see the ball bounce off the mannequin's capsule. That's because the capsule's data is used in both the physics and the query trees (data structures used for calculating query and physics interactions, respectively).

Probe Only (Contact Data, No Query or Physics Collision

While this setting may seem similar to Physics Only, it's not. With this setting, physics interactions don't occur (one ball won't bounce off another). But hit callbacks can be triggered in response to physics simulations. For this to occur, the Simulation Generates Hit Events Boolean must be set to true for this component.

Query and Probe (Query Collision and Contact Data, No Physics Collision)

We get probing behavior, i.e. hit callbacks triggered in response to physics simulations, but no physics collision. With this option, we also get queries. This includes ray casts, sweeps, and overlaps. While physics interactions will not occur, contact data will still be generated (hit callbacks can be triggered).

The Collision Enabled property is one of the defining characteristics of a component's collision profile, and the choice you make for this property is an important one. One mistake many developers make is to enable more than they need to (i.e. enable queries when all they needed was physics, or enable physics when all they needed was queries, or enable physics when they only needed hit events to trigger).

While over-enabling your component results in a less-than-optimized setup, it is still not the biggest cause for confusion in the collision framework. The biggest cause for confusion I've seen is the collision Object Type, coupled with the Collision Responses in a component's collision profile. We'll talk about these next.

Collision Object Type

A component's collision profile includes its Object Type. This is not to be confused with the component's class type (i.e. Static Mesh Component, Sphere Component, etc.). The collision Object Type is a collision channel chosen for a given component. Every component with collision has an Object Type, along with a set of Collision Responses to all the Object Types defined in the project. While you can add your own custom Object Types to your project, Object Types are limited in number for a project.

Collision Responses

A component's collision profile has a Collision Response to all collision Object Types, including its own collision Object Type. Collision Responses can each be one of three choices:

- Ignore

- Overlap

- Block

The Collision Responses above are listed in increasing order. Overlap is more blocking than Ignore, and Block is more blocking than Overlap. This order is significant when it comes to understanding how the Collision Responses tie into the concept of collision filtering.

Collision Presets

Unreal Engine allows for collision settings to be saved as named presets. There are several built-in Collision Presets, but custom presets can be made as well. A collision preset has the Collision Enabled, Object Type, and Collision Responses set and associated with a collision profile name. While the engine limits the number of collision Object Types a project can have, there is no such limitation on Collision Presets.

Collision Filtering

Collision filtering is how Unreal Engine's collision system decides what should happen when two objects interact based on their collision profiles. This is the very reason for each component having its own collision Object Type.

When one object with collision data (collision geometry and a collision profile) encounters another object with collision data, the resulting collision interaction is determined by the two objects' collision profiles.

Each collision profile has both an Object Type and a set of Collision Responses to all Object Types, as we've seen. To determine the resulting collision interaction, we must look at the Object Types and Responses for **both components**.

Example Collision Interaction

Let's consider an example. Let's say we have two Actors encountering one another in a game. For clarity's sake, we'll be specific.

We have a Blueprint called BP_Ball, based on the Actor class. BP_Ball has a single component, called Sphere, of type Static Mesh Component, designated as the Root Component of BP_Ball.

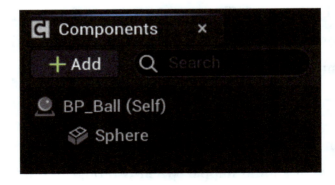

Figure 2.2 – BP_Ball's Components Panel

The Sphere Static Mesh Component has its Static Mesh property set to a Static Mesh called SM_Sphere.

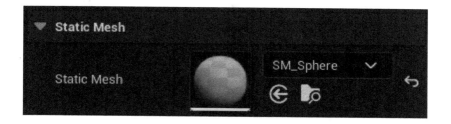

Figure 2.3 – Sphere's Static Mesh

And in the Static Mesh editor, SM_Sphere has its Collision Complexity set to Project Default, which, as we know, defaults to the setting in Project Settings for Default Shape Complexity, which is set to Simple and Complex.

The SM_Sphere Static Mesh has a sphere simple collision, added in the Static Mesh editor via Collision -> Add Sphere Simplified Collision.

In addition, in the Static Mesh editor, SM_Sphere has its Collision Presets set to Block All. This is a built-in preset in which the collision profile is filled in and cannot be changed. The settings for the Block All collision preset are shown in the following figure.

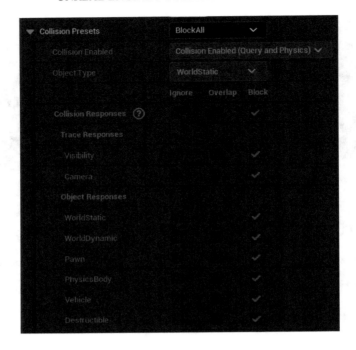

Figure 2.4 – Settings in the Block All Collision Preset

Now we've exactly described the collision situation. Why so much detail? Because it all matters. The hypothetical situation "two objects collide" is too vague to have any meaning. There's no way to determine the results of such an interaction. However, now we know the specifics: Two Actors, each with a single Static Mesh Component with collision data, come into contact. We know their collision profiles, as determined by the BlockAll collision preset:

- Each has Collision Enabled set to Collision Enabled (Query and Physics).

- Each has the Object Type WorldStatic (this means they are using the WorldStatic collision channel).

- Each has its Collision Responses set to Block for all collision channels.

Surely, we have enough information now to determine what should happen when these two objects meet, don't we?

Actually, we don't.

There's one last question: *how are the objects moving?*

The resulting collision interaction depends entirely on the answer to this question. In particular, we must know if the object is moved using physics. And if not, we must know if the object is moved using sweeping.

You may open the Static Mesh editor for this SM_Sphere asset, look at its Collision Presets and see that Collision Enabled is set to Collision Enabled (Query and Physics) and say "of course, the object is using physics!" But this is not necessarily true. The Collision Enabled setting has nothing to do with whether the component is using physics. It just means that collisions *can* be registered *if* the component is using physics.

So, we must know if the objects are moving via physics or some other means. For this hypothetical example, let's say we look at the Details panel for the Sphere Static Mesh Component, and under Physics, we see that Simulate Physics is set to true (the checkbox is checked). And for additional clarity, we'll say that Enable Gravity is set to false (it's unchecked) as shown in the following figure.

Figure 2.5 – Physics Settings for Sphere

So physics is enabled, and gravity is disabled. How will these Actors encounter each other, then? Well, we can apply forces to move them.

First, we'll orient them such that they face each other. Then, on **Begin Play**, we'll add a force in the direction of the forward vector of BP_Ball.

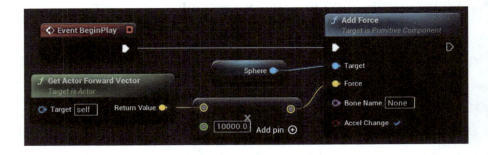

Figure 2.6 – Adding a Force to the Sphere Component

Here, checking **Accel Change** in **Add Force** allows us to apply this force in the form of an acceleration change, not taking the mass of the component into account.

Now, do we finally have enough information to determine what will happen when these two objects interact?

We do! As you no doubt have guessed, the objects will bounce off each other. They bounce because opposing forces are imparted on each object as a result of the physics collision. This result would not be possible if the Sphere Static Mesh Component on each BP_Actor were not configured to use physics. Each has its Collision Enabled setting set to Collision Enbaled (Query and Physics). It's the "Physics" part in that setting that allows for this blocking interaction to occur. In fact, if we were to try changing Collision Enabled to anything other than Query and Physics or Physics Only, we would be met with the following Blueprint runtime warnings in the Message Log:

Invalid Simulate Options: Body (BP_Ball.Sphere SM_Sphere) is set to simulate physics but Collision Enabled is incompatible.

BP_Ball.Sphere SM_Sphere has to have 'CollisionEnabled' set to 'Query and Physics' or 'Physics Only' if you'd like to AddForce.

The first message is due to the incompatibility between Simulate Physics being true while Collision Enabled does not allow for physics.

The second message is due to the call to Add Force in the

Blueprint Event Graph while Collision Enabled does not allow for physics.

This type of collision interaction would also not be possible had the Simulate Physics checkbox been unchecked in the Details panel for the Sphere Static Mesh Component in BP_Ball. If we uncheck Simulate Physics (and keep Collision Enabled set to Query and Physics), we will be met with the following Blueprint runtime warning:

```
BP_Ball.Sphere SM_Sphere has to have 'Simulate
Physics' enabled if you'd like to AddForce.
```

This is due to the call to **Add Force** being made while the component is not simulating physics.

This is a very specific type of interaction. As you can see, we had to specify quite a few characteristics to fully determine the outcome. If we were to change just one of these characteristics, the outcome would be different. Let's explore.

Let's say we'd like to move the object in a different way. Instead of using forces, we'd like to add a world offset using the **Add Actor World Offset** function.

This function does not use physics. In fact, we can disable Simulate Physics for the Sphere Static Mesh Component entirely (we'll do that by unchecking Simulate Physics as in the following figure).

Figure 2.7 - Disabling Physics on the Sphere

In Tick, we'll use **Add Actor World Offset** using the Actor forward vector (this will move the Actor by a fixed amount each frame, which is frame-rate dependent, but it will suffice for this example).

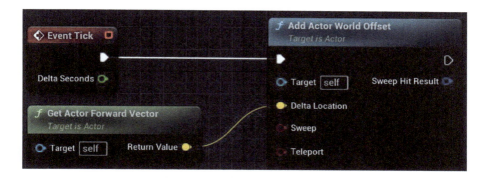

Figure 2.8 - Adding a World Offset to BP_Ball

Since we know that the BP_Ball has Sphere as the Root Component, this offset will be applied to the Sphere Static Mesh Component. And since these Actors are facing each other, they'll approach each other until they meet.

So, what will be the result of this interaction? Well, notice the Boolean input Sweep on the **Add Actor World Offset** node in Figure 2.8. That checkbox is unchecked, so we're passing in false there. This will result in the two BP_Ball Actors passing through each other!

You may feel like this interaction doesn't make sense—it's a direct contradiction to the objects' Block responses to each other's collision Object Types. But it's a testament to the fact that *the way we move the objects matters.*

Add Actor World Offset is directly setting the location of the Actor, specified by an Offset vector. If that location happens to mean that one or more components of the Actor interpenetrates with a component on another Actor, so be it. We're setting the location directly. Without physics imparting forces on the objects, there is nothing preventing them from overlapping with each other. Now, enable physics for the Sphere Static Mesh Component once again. Play testing, we find that the objects no longer pass through one another, because they now impart opposing forces as soon as they come into contact.

Add Actor World Offset is working against physics, here. If we add just such an offset that the two Sphere meshes interpenetrate, the spheres will impart forces on each other, pushing each other away until they are no longer overlapping.

Attempting to place one component in the same location as another, when both are set to block each other's collision Object Types, and both are simulating physics, is an error. To attempt to do so is to demonstrate a lack of understanding of the collision system in Unreal Engine, and this is the type of situation that leads to bugs.

When a component is simulating physics, the physics system uses forces to move it. When you attempt to manually set its location via functions like **Add Actor World Offset**, **Set Actor Location**, **Set World Location** (for components), etc., you are conflicting with the physics system. If a component is simulating physics, and you move it with forces, you are acting within the physics system.

Now, let's set Simulate Physics to false on the Sphere once again (uncheck it). In **Tick**, we'll still move the Actor forward, except this time, we'll pass a value of true into the **Add Actor World Offset** input pin titled **Sweep** (we'll check the checkbox).

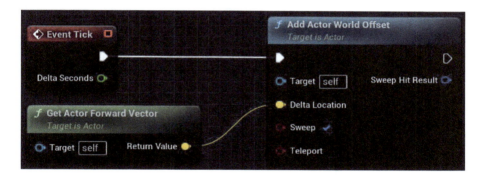

Figure 2.9 – Adding a World Offset with Sweeping

What will happen this time? The spheres will not pass through each other, and the spheres aren't even simulating physics! This time, the blocking behavior we see has nothing to do with the physics system. The key difference here is that we're *sweeping*.

Sweeping

Sweeping depends on a component's ability to perform spatial queries. Because our Sphere Static Mesh Component has its Collision Enabled setting set to Collision Enabled (Query and Physics), we can perform spatial queries (this is the "Query" part of "Query and Physics").

Sweeping involves moving a shape from one location to another and seeing if collision would occur at any point between the original location and the new location. If there is nothing in the way, the object moves from location 1 to location 2 without any problems (see the following figure).

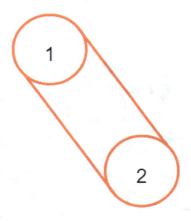

Figure 2.10 – Sweeping Without a Collision

However, if there is blocking geometry along the way, the moving object stops short of that blocking geometry.

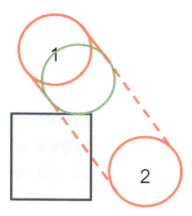

Figure 2.11 – Sweeping With a Collision

This means that, even though we are attempting to set the object's location directly, the object fails to reach that intended destination because a blocking collision was detected along the way. This blocking interaction is detected by the spatial query system and *not* the physics system in Unreal Engine.

So, as we can see, the outcome of a collision interaction depends on the way we are moving the objects involved. This is true even when the two objects have the same exact collision profiles (as they do in our example in this chapter).

In general, objects can be moved either via the physics system (with forces), or without physics (setting the location directly). When moved without physics, we must then consider whether sweeping is involved.

You may be thinking that there's another way to move objects. What about Movement Components? What if you're moving a projectile Actor via the use of a Projectile Movement Component? Or running with a Character using a Character Movement Component?

Movement Components are a more sophisticated way to move objects in Unreal Engine. They are based on the Movement Component class (UMovementComponent in C++) and they handle updating the position of their Updated Component.

The Projectile Movement Component, for example, checks to see if its Updated Component is simulating physics. If so, only the initial launch parameters set in the Projectile Movement Component will affect the projectile, provided that the initial velocity is not set to zero. After the initial launch, the Projectile Movement Component hands the movement over to the physics simulation. So, if you launch a component that has a Projectile Movement Component, and that component is also simulating physics, then when it hits another object, we'll observe the same outcome as if the object had been launched via forces (as with Add Force).

If the Updated Component is not simulating physics however, we'll observe the same result as if we were updating the location manually (as with Add Actor World Offset) and sweeping will occur (though it can be disabled via the Blueprint-exposed Boolean called bSweepCollision, editable in the Details panel as Sweep Collision).

So, when it comes to determining what should result from a collision interaction with a component being moved via a Movement Component, it's necessary to look at the settings of the component itself as well as the settings on the Movement Component.

As we can see, analyzing collision requires a great deal of information. Not only do we need to know the collision profiles of the bodies involved, but we must also know how they're being moved. Our example was an easy one, though. Both objects were set to block each other's collision Object Types. What happens when we have two objects whose Collision Responses to each other's collision channels are different? It is crucial to understand how to determine the outcome of such cases, and we'll discuss that next.

3 – COLLISION FILTERING IN DETAIL

As we know, a component with collision has its own collision profile, consisting of Collision Enabled, a collision Object Type, and Collision Responses. The collision Object Type and Collision Responses form the basis for collision filtering.

This is the most important aspect of the Unreal Engine collision framework, so listen up. If you pay attention to any one part of this book, pay attention to this one.

When two objects meet, we look at each object's collision Object Type and its response to the other object's collision Object Type, then take the *least blocking* of the two responses.

That's how we determine the type of collision interaction that will result. Remember back in Chapter 2, when we learned that the three collision responses were Ignore, Overlap, and Block, and that these were listed in ascending order? Remember that Block is more blocking than Overlap, and that Overlap is more blocking than Ignore?

That's how we determine the *least blocking* of two given responses.

The following table may help you to visualize the result of a collision interaction between Object A and Object B, based on their responses to each other's collision Object Types.

Object A

	Ignore	Overlap	Block
Ignore	Ignore	Ignore	Ignore
Overlap	Ignore	Overlap	Overlap
Block	Ignore	Overlap	Block

Object B

Table 3.1 - Collision Interaction Based on Mutual Responses

From Table 3.1, we can determine the type of collision interaction that occurs between Object A and Object B. First, we find Object A's response to Object B's collision Object Type in the topmost row of emboldened responses. We then move down that column until we find the row corresponding to Object B's response to Object A's collision Object Type. The intersecting square is the resulting type of interaction.

Notice that if one object's response to the other's type is Ignore, the resulting type of interaction will be Ignore, no matter what the other object's responses are. If one object's response to the other's Object Type is Block, we only get a blocking interaction if the other object's response to the first is Block as well.

Let's solidify this with an example. We'll consider the Capsule

Component on our third-person Character and its collision interactions with two objects in our level: a bush, and a wall.

Figure 3.1 – A Character, a Bush, and a Wall

We are moving the Character via the Character Movement Component, which means the Character Movement Component is setting the location of the Character and sweeping is involved (this is how the Character Movement Component moves its owning Character's Root Component.). For simplicity's sake, we won't consider any collision interactions with the Character's mesh.

Note that the bush in the above figure is from the Unreal Engine Starter Content. As there is no default collision geometry on this bush, for the purposes of this exercise, a collision hull was added to the bush in the Static Mesh editor via Collision -> Add 18DOP Simplified Collision.

Figure 3.2 - 18DOP Simplified Collision on the Bush

So, what other information do we need? We need to know the collision Object Types of the three objects involved, and their responses to the other object's Object Types. Let's lay them out.

The Capsule Component on the Character has the following Object Type and responses:

Object Type: *Pawn*

Responses	
Pawn	Block
WorldStatic	Block

Table 3.2 - Capsule Component Type and Responses

The bush has the following Object Type and responses:

*Object Type: **WorldStatic***

Responses	
Pawn	Overlap
WorldStatic	Block

Table 3.3 – Bush Type and Responses

The wall has the following Object Type and responses:

*Object Type: **WorldStatic***

Responses	
Pawn	Block
WorldStatic	Block

Table 3.4 – Wall Type and Responses

Do you think you can figure out the types of collision interactions that will result when the Character runs toward the bush and wall?

Let's first consider the interaction between the Character and the bush. The Capsule Component on the Character has collision Object Type Pawn, and the bush has collision Object Type WorldStatic.

The Capsule Component's response to WorldStatic is Block, and the bush's response to Pawn is Overlap. Looking at Table 3.1, we see that Overlap is the resulting interaction. The Character will pass through the bush.

Now let's consider the interaction between the Character and the wall.

The Capsule Component's response to WorldStatic is Block, and the wall's response to Pawn is Block. Looking at Table 3.1, we see that Block is the resulting interaction. The Character will hit the wall and stop.

You may be thinking: "what's the difference between Ignore and Overlap? Don't they result in the same thing?"

While the Character's interaction with the bush resulted in an Overlap, this is not the same as an Ignore interaction. The difference between these interactions is not one that you can see while testing this example. It's much more subtle than that. Overlap and Block interactions both involve calculations to detect them, and result in collision callbacks – a subject we'll discuss now.

4 – COLLISION CALLBACKS

The Unreal Engine collision framework allows for callbacks to result from collision interactions. These are very important features that allow us to implement gameplay mechanics in response to interactions between objects in our games.

Overlap and Block interactions trigger these callbacks, provided that the interacting components are configured properly.

In our previous example with the Character, the bush, and the wall, the interaction between the Character and the bush was an Overlap interaction. This provides us with the opportunity to test overlap collision callbacks.

Overlap Callbacks

The Primitive Component class has two delegates related to overlaps: OnComponentBeginOverlap and OnComponentEndOverlap. These delegates can have functions bound to them which will be called in response to an Overlap interaction with the Primitive Component that owns the delegates.

On Component Begin Overlap

The Primitive Component's OnComponentBeginOverlap delegate can be bound to in C++ or in Blueprint. The callback function must have the appropriate function signature to be bound to it. In C++, the function signature is as follows:

```
UFUNCTION()
void OnOverlap(
    UPrimitiveComponent* OverlappedComponent,
    AActor* OtherActor,
    UPrimitiveComponent* OtherComp,
    int32 OtherBodyIndex,
    bool bFromSweep,
    const FHitResult& SweepResult);
```

The function name doesn't matter, but the input parameters and return type do. Notice the UFUNCTION macro; this is required for the callback, as this particular flavor of delegate requires it (it's a dynamic multicast delegate).

Binding the Callback in C++

To bind the callback to the OnComponentBeginOverlap delegate in C++, AddDynamic is called, passing in the user object and address to the callback. The following demonstrates how to bind the function OnOverlap to the OnComponentBeginOverlap delegate on the Comp variable:

```
Comp->OnComponentBeginOverlap.AddDynamic(
    this,
    &ThisClass::OnOverlap);
```

Binding the Callback in Blueprint

These delegates are reflected in Blueprint, and we can assign events as callbacks to them. There is a **Bind** function that can have an event hooked into its event input:

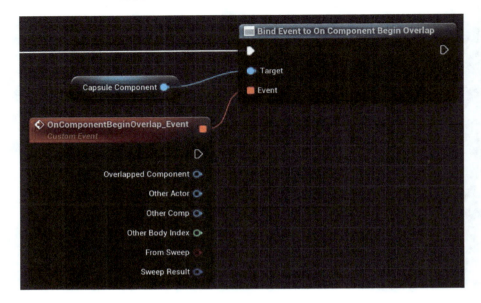

Figure 4.1 – Assigning an Event to On Component Begin Overlap

When an Overlap interaction occurs, the custom event hooked into **Bind Event to On Component Begin Overlap** will be called, and we have access to the same six parameters we saw in the C++ callback function signature above:

- **Overlapped Component** – The component this delegate belongs to.

- **Other Actor** – The other Actor that overlapped with this component.

- **Other Comp** – The other component that overlapped with this component.

- **Other Body Index** – The bone index that the overlapped Physics Body corresponds to on the Physics Asset if overlapping with a Skeletal Mesh Component

- **From Sweep** – True if this overlap was the result of sweeping movement.
- **Sweep Result** – Hit Result containing information about the hit resulting from sweeping. Only valid if sweeping was involved.

For overlap callbacks to be called, both interacting components must have their Generate Overlap Events Boolean set to true. This Boolean is exposed to the Details panel in Blueprint.

We can verify that the overlap callback is being called by printing a debug message. If our Character is based on the ACharacter class, we can set its Capsule Component's Generate Overlap Events Boolean to true in the Character's constructor:

```
GetCapsuleComponent()-
>SetGenerateOverlapEvents(true);
```

Then we can bind our OnOverlap callback to the Capsule Component's OnComponentBeginOverlap delegate in BeginPlay (don't bind this in the constructor—this would bind the callback on the Class Default Object too and we don't want callbacks bound on that).

```
GetCapsuleComponent()-
>OnComponentBeginOverlap.AddDynamic(
    this,
```

```
&ThisClass::OnOverlap);
```

Next, we'll simply print a debug message in OnOverlap. Since we have access to information involved in the overlap, we might as well print some of it! The following is our implementation of OnOverlap.

```
void ACollisionCharacter::OnOverlap(
    UPrimitiveComponent* OverlappedComponent,
    AActor* OtherActor,
    UPrimitiveComponent* OtherComp,
    int32 OtherBodyIndex,
    bool bFromSweep,
    const FHitResult& SweepResult)
{
    FString Message =
FString::Format(TEXT("Overlapped with: {0}"),
{OtherActor->GetName()});

    GEngine->AddOnScreenDebugMessage(
    -1,
    30.f,
    FColor::Red,
    Message);
}
```

In OnOverlap, we are simply getting the OtherActor and calling GetName on it, then adding an onscreen debug message to display it.

We'll do the same thing in Blueprint with a **Print String** node. In Blueprint, we call the exposed **Get Object Name** function to retrieve the **OtherActor**'s name:

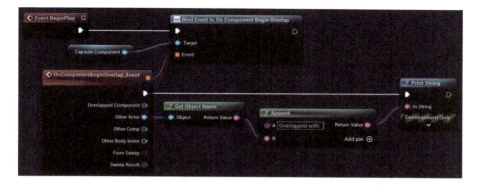

Figure 4.2 - Printing Other Actor's Name in Blueprint

And to ensure that our overlap results in these callbacks being called, we must ensure that the bush Static Mesh has its Generate Overlap Events Boolean set to true. This Boolean does not exist on Static Mesh assets, so it cannot be done in the Static Mesh editor. Once a Static Mesh has been dragged into the Level, however, a Static Mesh Actor is automatically created for it, which has a Static Mesh Component. Since Static Mesh Components are Primitive Components, they inherit the collision settings and properties exposed by the Primitive Component class. So, we can select the bush Static Mesh Actor in the Level and search for its Generate Overlap Events Boolean and check its checkbox.

Figure 4.3 - Generate Overlap Events for the Bush

If this bush came straight out of Starter Content, it likely has its Collision Presets set to Default. For testing purposes, we can change it to Custom… (and remind ourselves that we'll soon learn why this is not the best practice). Now we can set its response to Pawn to Overlap.

Figure 4.4 – Bush's response to Pawn: Overlap

We must also ensure that the Character's Capsule Component has its Generate Overlap Events Boolean set to true. A quick check will show that it's true by default. Notice that by default, the Capsule Component's response to WorldStatic (the bush's collision Object Type) is set to Block. The least blocking between Overlap and Block is Overlap, which will be the resulting interaction.

Now, we can test our callbacks by running into the bush. We will see that we get two messages printed to the screen: one from our C++ callback, and one from our custom event we bound in Blueprint.

An alternative to using the **Bind Event to On Component Begin Overlap** node in the Event Graph is to use the ready-made event called **On Component Begin Overlap (CapsuleComponent)**, which gives the same result.

Figure 4.5 – On Component Begin Overlap (CapsuleComponent)

Now, I know you're dying to know more about the other parameters. Particularly, that **Sweep Result**. We're moving the Character via the Character Movement Component, after all, and we've already established that it moves the Character using sweeps. So, shall we access more of this juicy data?

We'll once again use FString::Format to package up data from the first five parameters into one neat message. For the Hit Result, we'll draw a couple of debug shapes: a sphere at the Impact Point, and an arrow depicting the Impact Normal. The following will go inside our OnOverlap callback. First, our message:

```
FString Message = FString::Format(
    TEXT("{0}, {1} {2}, {3}, {4}"),
    {
        OverlappedComponent->GetName(),
        OtherActor->GetName(),
        OtherComp->GetName(),
        OtherBodyIndex,
        bFromSweep
    });
```

Next, our call to `AddOnScreenDebugMessage`. We are drawing the message with key -1 (no key) for 30 seconds with color red.

```
GEngine->AddOnScreenDebugMessage(
    -1,
    30.f,
    FColor::Red,
    Message);
```

Next, the debug sphere. We are drawing the sphere at the Impact Point with a radius of 10, segments 12, color red, false for persistent lines, and a duration of 30 seconds.

```
DrawDebugSphere(
    GetWorld(),
    SweepResult.ImpactPoint,
    10.f,
    12,
    FColor::Red,
    false,
    30.f);
```

And finally, the debug arrow. We start the arrow at the Impact Point, and end the arrow 25 units out in the Impact Normal direction. We have arrow size 10, color red, duration 30 seconds, and thickness 3.

```
UKismetSystemLibrary::DrawDebugArrow(
    this,
    SweepResult.ImpactPoint,
    SweepResult.ImpactPoint +
SweepResult.ImpactNormal * 25.f,
    10.f, FLinearColor::Red,
    30.f,
```

```
3.f);
```

The following figure shows the result after running through the bush three times. We get the red spheres at the Impact Point for each overlap interaction, and the arrows depict the Impact Normal for those overlaps.

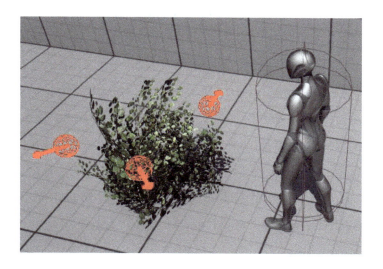

Figure 4.6 – Results of the Overlap Interaction

Our debug message displays:

```
Collision      Cylinder,      StaticMeshActor_X,
StaticMeshComponent0, -1, 1
```

These results can be summarized as follows:

- OverlappedComponent is Collision Cylinder (the Capsule Component belonging to our Character)

- OtherActor is StaticMeshActor_X (the bush Static

Mesh Actor)

- `OtherComp` is `StaticMeshComponent0` (the Static Mesh Component on the bush Static Mesh Actor)

- `OtherBodyIndex` is `-1` (because the bush has no corresponding bone index, as it has no Skeleton and no Physics Asset)

- `bFromSweep` is 1 (the Boolean true converted to string via `FString::Format`)

We can achieve the same result in Blueprint, of course. We can simply use the **Append** node for strings to concatenate the parameters, each converted to a string. The **Sweep Result** needs a **Break Hit Result** node, and the **Impact Point** and **Impact Normal** can be retrieved from that. The following figure shows the resulting nodes, utilizing the single **On Component Begin Overlap (CapsuleComponent)** event node for the implementation.

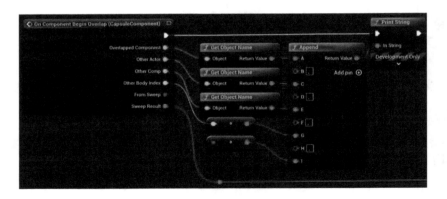

Figure 4.7 – Overlap Interaction, pt. 1

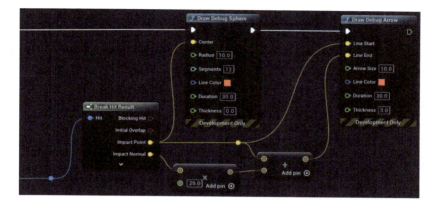

Figure 4.8 - Overlap Interaction, pt. 2

Overlap callbacks have access to a good deal of information, as we can see. Note that the Hit Result **Sweep Result** will not be populated with any meaningful data if the overlap does not result from a sweep.

The Primitive Component class also has an OnComponentEndOverlap delegate that behaves similarly, except that it is broadcast when the component stops overlapping with another object. The interaction will only be registered if the collision settings of the interacting components are configured to register overlaps, just as is the case with OnComponentBeginOverlap. The input parameters and their types for this callback can be seen by assigning an event to this delegate in Blueprint. You can also get this information by investigating the delegate declarations for these delegates in the PrimitiveComponent.h header file.

Actor Begin Overlap

If you've ever created an Actor Blueprint, you've probably noticed (and been annoyed by) the three grayed-out events in the Actor Blueprint's Event Graph. These are Begin Play, Tick, and Actor Begin Overlap.

Begin Play and Tick are commonly used events. What about Actor Begin Overlap?

This is a delegate on the Actor class. It will be called in response to overlap interactions with any

Figure 4.9 – The Grayed-out Events

component on the Actor, provided that all components involved are configured to register overlap events with one another.

For example, let's say we were to create a new Actor Blueprint and add a Sphere Component. A Sphere Component has the OverlapAllDynamic collision preset by default. It also has Generate Overlap Events set to true by default. If we add a Print String to the Actor Begin Overlap event on this Actor, we will print the message in response to overlaps with this Sphere Component.

Something to keep in mind is that **Actor Begin Overlap** (and its counterpart, **Actor End Overlap**) are called in response to overlap events on the Actor as a whole. This means that if the Actor has multiple components that are configured to overlap, and more than one of them overlaps with another component, **Actor Begin Overlap** treats all components on the Actor as one entity.

For example, if a Character's Skeletal Mesh Component and the Character's Capsule Component both overlap with the Sphere Component, **Actor Begin Overlap** will only trigger once, since it only considers Actors as a whole, rather than individual components for overlaps. This gives less fine-tuned control over the overlap interactions that occur between Components. Events **Actor Begin Overlap** and **Actor End Overlap** are easy to use (as are the Shape Components) but that doesn't mean they're ideal for real games in all scenarios. The collision preset OverlapAllDynamic, for example, is configured to register overlap interactions with all other collision Object Types. While this makes it easy to add a Shape Component to an Actor and quickly get overlap events firing, it's rarely something you'd want in a real game (if ever).

Hit Callbacks

Hit callbacks result from blocking interactions. These can result from two objects blocking each other's collision Object

Types, though they need not physically block each other. Two objects can be set to block each other's Object Types yet have their Collision Enabled setting configured to probe, which will register hit interactions without the blocking nature of physics (forces keeping objects from penetrating and imparting impulses on each other).

On Component Hit

The OnComponentHit delegate on the Primitive Component class is broadcast in response to blocking interactions. The proper signature for a C++ function callback that can be bound to this delegate is as follows:

```
UFUNCTION()
void OnHit(
    UPrimitiveComponent* HitComponent,
    AActor* OtherActor,
    UPrimitiveComponent* OtherComp,
    FVector NormalImpulse,
    const FHitResult& Hit);
```

Such a callback has access to the hit component, the other Actor, the other component, the normal impulse, and a Hit Result containing information regarding the hit.

For a hit callback to be called, a blocking interaction must be registered. There are several scenarios that will suffice.

The object can be moved in several possible ways.

Manually Setting Location

Using functions like **Add Actor World Offset** and **Set Actor Location**, sweeping must be used in order to trigger hit callbacks. If sweeping, hit callbacks will be called even if both objects are not simulating physics. In this situation, the hit callback is a result of queries, and Collision Enabled must be set up to register queries. This means any of the following will suffice:

- Query Only (No Physics Collision)

- Collision Enabled (Query and Physics)

- Query and Probe (Query Collision and Contact Data, No Physics Collision)

In this case, the hit interaction is a result of queries, which is why hit callbacks are called despite our components not simulating physics at all.

Adding Force

To move our components via forces, they must be simulating physics. A blocking interaction will result as long as both components have their Collision Enabled setting configured to register physics interactions. Any of the following will suffice:

- Physics Only (No Query Collision)

- Collision Enabled (Query and Physics)

- Probe Only (Contact Data, No Query or Physics Collision)

- Query and Probe (Query Collision and Contact Data, No Physics Collision)

Both components must have at least Physics Only (No Query Collision) or Collision Enabled (Query and Physics) in order for the objects to stop each other, otherwise they will pass through each other. If at least one of the components has its Collision Enabled set to Probe Only (Contact Data, No Query or Physics Collision) or Query and Probe (Query Collision and Contact Data, No Physics Collision), the objects will pass through one another, yet still trigger hit callbacks.

If the objects both have Collision Enabled set to Physics Only (No Query Collision) or Collision Enabled (Query and Physics), the objects will bounce off each other, due to a normal impulse. This is the situation that will result in a non-zero normal impulse in the callback's input parameter `NormalImpulse`. Otherwise, `NormalImpulse` will be a zero vector.

Movement Component

Moving the object via a Movement Component depends on whether the object is simulating physics or moving via sweeping. We get similar results to the above scenarios in each respective case.

Caution

Use caution when implementing hit callbacks. These will trigger every frame if the components remain in contact.

Observe the following result when drawing debug spheres at the Impact Point of a hit event when a third-person Character slides along the surface of a wall:

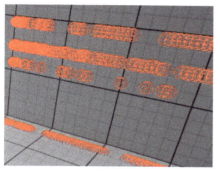

Overlap and hit callbacks are useful for testing collision interactions because we can print debug messages and draw debug shapes in response to overlap and hit events. This allows for experimentation and clarification when investigating the Unreal Engine collision framework.

Figure 4.10 – Hit Events with a Wall

5 – COLLISION CHANNELS

Unreal Engine has two types of collision channels—Trace Channels and Object Channels.

A component with a collision profile has a collision Object Type. This is a collision channel assigned to that component. Components with collision can only be assigned one of the Object Channels. Trace Channels are reserved for traces.

Collision channels identify the type of object involved in a collision interaction. They allow objects to differentiate between one another to decide the type of collision interaction that should occur. Every object with collision must decide how to interact with every collision Object Channel and Trace Channel.

Unreal Engine has a number of built-in collision channels. Some (but not all) are the following:

Trace Channels

- Visibility

- Camera

Object Channels

- WorldStatic

- WorldDynamic

- Pawn

- PhysicsBody

- Vehicle

- Destructible

Notice that there were no descriptions next to the channels listed above. So then, what is each channel designated for? What do the channels mean?

The answer is that it's the responsibility of the team making the game to decide what each channel means. I've found that many developers are unsure of what each collision channel should be used for, and many are confused when deciding on a channel for a component and its responses to the collision channels.

Visibility, for example, is an often-misunderstood collision channel. It's a trace channel, and many developers opt for this channel for all line traces. Does Visibility pertain to all things that are visible? Or is it a sort of "catch-all" collision channel that everything should block?

The answer is that it's up to your team to decide what Visibility means. The Visibility collision channel has no relationship to render visibility whatsoever. Even objects that are hidden in-game can be set to block the Visibility channel.

It's recommended for a team to have a predefined list or chart that maps out the collision channels and their uses. The team should consistently stick to these conventions for the project.

This can greatly reduce the amount of confusion when deciding on a collision channel for a given component, as well as the responses that a component should have to all the channels.

Custom Collision Channels

Custom Trace Channels and Object Channels can be added to your project from within the Project Settings. There is a limited number of custom channels that can be added to a project (18 total custom channels), so the decision to add a new collision channel should not be made lightly.

Go to Edit -> Project Settings -> Engine -> Collision to access options for creating new collision channels.

An example scenario in which you may want to create a new channel is for foot IK (inverse kinematics).

Example Custom Trace Channel: FootIK

Let's say you are part of a team that has started a game project using the third-person template project as a starting point.

The third-person template project comes with a third-person Character and a Control Rig for foot IK. As of Unreal Engine version 5.4.1, the Control Rig asset for foot IK exists in the Content folder under Characters -> Mannequins -> Rigs -> CR_Mannequin_BasicFootIK.

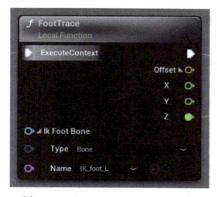

Figure 5.1 – FootTrace in the Control Rig

This Control Rig works by performing a sphere trace from the IK bones on the Character's Skeleton downwards. The trace result is then used to move the feet downward, so they are positioned on the ground. The tracing takes place in the **FootTrace** function.

The **Start** and **End** locations for the sphere trace are above and below the specified IK bone, as can be seen in the function.

The sphere trace is performed via the **Sphere Trace By Trace Channel** function. This trace uses the Visibility channel, as can be see in **Figure 5.2**.

The **Sphere Trace By Trace Channel** is a query that requires a Trace Channel. By default, Unreal Engine has two trace channels: Visibility, and Camera. The Visibility channel is selected for this trace. This means

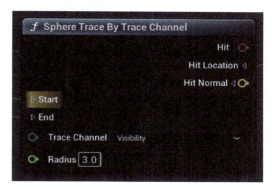

Figure 5.2 – Sphere Trace By Trace Channel

that any components that are configured to block the Visibility channel will register a trace hit with this trace.

Since the ground and other obstacles in the game project are configured to block the Visibility channel, this gives a nice effect when the Control Rig moves the feet of the mannequin such that they are positioned on top of blocking objects.

Figure 5.3 - FootIK on a Ramp

However, let's say the project develops into a more complex game, and the team soon realizes that this trace against the Visibility channel has become problematic. One of the problems is that the foot trace is hitting the Skeletal Mesh Components of other Characters in the game. The game may be using the Visibility channel for other traces, such as those performed by weapons. So, Character meshes can't stop blocking the Visibility channel.

The result of this sphere trace hitting other Character's Skeletal Mesh Components results in the Character's foot being placed on the legs of nearby Characters, as shown in the following figure.

Figure 5.4 – Side Effects of Using the Visibility Channel

It has been decided by the team that this leg placement is unwanted, and a plan must be devised to prevent it.

Since the foot trace in the Control Rig requires a trace channel, the only options available are Visibility and Camera. It doesn't make sense to assign the Camera channel to a sphere trace used for foot IK, so the team decides that this warrants the creation of a new collision channel. You are assigned this task.

The way you decide to fix this problem is by creating a new trace channel called FootIK. The default response to this channel for all collision profiles will be Block. Here is the process you take:

Figure 5.5 – Creation of the FootIK Channel

In Project Settings -> Engine -> Collision -> Trace Channels, you select New Trace Channel... and name the new channel FootIK, setting its Default Response to Block.

Now, a new trace channel exists in your project called FootIK, and all objects with collision profiles now have the responsibility to choose a collision response to this new channel. By default, all collision profiles in the game project will have their response to FootIK set to Block.

Now, you can go into your Control Rig and assign the FootIK channel to your sphere trace:

Figure 5.6 – Using the FootIK Trace Channel

For most objects in the game, Block is the appropriate response to this channel. However, Character Skeletal Mesh Components need to have their response to this channel set to Ignore.

Figure 5.7 – Ignoring the FootIK Channel

With this change, Character Skeletal Mesh Components ignore the foot trace, and the Character's leg is no longer placed on top of other Characters' legs.

Figure 5.8 – Proper Foot IK Behavior

Creating a new trace channel has allowed for a more specific type of interaction— that with traces performed specifically for foot IK. Other types of traces, such as those performed for weapons, can still use their own trace channels, and components that are configured to block those channels can still block them, while now ignoring the FootIK channel. It's important to keep in mind though that not all objects in the game will necessarily be appropriate for blocking this channel. Overlap volumes such as Sphere and Box

Components, for example, would likely want to ignore this channel.

This brings up an important point when it comes to custom collision channels: **Creating a new collision channel is always a big deal.** Every time you make a new channel, all collision profiles must now decide how to interact with that channel. Depending on the size of the game project, this may require adjusting a large number of assets, especially if many components are using the Custom... collision preset.

DefaultEngine.ini

When you create a new collision channel in Project Settings, a new line is added to `[/Script/Engine.CollisionProfile]` in `DefaultEngine.ini`:

```
+DefaultChannelResponses=(Channel=ECC_GameTrac
eChannel1,DefaultResponse=ECR_Block,bTraceType
=True,bStaticObject=False,Name="FootIK")
```

Notice that this line assigns `ECC_GameTraceChannel1` the name `FootIK`. This means that the new custom channel FootIK is actually the collision channel called `ECC_GameTraceChannel1` in native C++ code. It is simply displayed as FootIK in the editor. For this reason, many developers create a macro symbol for the new collision channel for clarity.

```
#define ECC_FootIK ECC_GameTraceChannel1
```

This allows for the new custom channel to be used in C++ by the name ECC_FootIK without having to remember that ECC_GameTraceChannel1 is the channel designated for foot IK traces.

Since we cannot create new collision channels indefinitely, we must do so sparingly. But games are complex, and there are a large number of types of interactions! How are we supposed to make complex games without a large number of collision channels?

It is useful to keep the number of collision channels to a minimum, since creating a new one requires all collision profiles in the game to respond to that new channel.

To get a variety of different behaviors without creating many collision channels, we can make use of Collision Presets.

6 – CUSTOM COLLISION PRESETS

Collision Presets are collision profiles that have been associated with a profile name. These are great for setting up the collision profile for a specific type of object in a game.

To create a custom collision preset, go to **Project Settings -> Engine -> Collision -> Preset**. Here, the Collision Presets are visible and you can click on **New...** to create a new one.

A collision preset consists of a Name, Collision Enabled, a collision Object Type, and a Description. The built-in presets provide some default collision settings and descriptions that explain when you might want to use them. If these presets don't suit your needs properly, you can change the settings for each built-in preset here in **Project Settings** with the **Edit...** button.

Just because a built-in preset exists doesn't mean it's a good idea to use it. OverlapAllDynamic and OverlapAll have their responses to all channels set to Overlap. While this makes it easy to test overlap events, it's not a good preset for performance. Rarely, if ever, would you need a component to have Overlap interactions with *everything in the game.*

One mistake that many developers make is to set the Collision Presets for components on many Actors in their game to Custom... and tweak individual collision settings on a per-Actor basis. I've made this mistake myself many times. The reason this is a bad idea is because those Actors no longer have a defined set of collision settings that can be consistently reapplied to other Actors that need the same settings. When things don't work, it's now necessary to inspect each individual setting to find which one is incorrect, and this must be done on a per-Actor basis. Two different rock assets may have completely different Collision Presets, and when comparing the two, it's difficult to know which one is correct.

If, instead of using Custom... for components, custom presets are used for each category of collision object, debugging collision issues becomes orders of magnitude easier. It's now only necessary to find the incorrect setting on the preset rather than per Actor. Once a preset is fixed, all Actors using that preset are also fixed.

While you only get a limited number of collision channels, you can have an unlimited number of Collision Presets. You incur no additional runtime overhead for having a large number of Collision Presets. You can even have multiple Collision Presets with different names but identical collision settings, i.e. Rock and Wall, etc.

Example Custom Preset: BlockPlayerOnly

Let's say you need certain objects to interact only with the player-controlled Character. For instance, you may need a blocking collision volume preventing the player from venturing out of bounds in a Level, but NPCs, projectiles, and other Actors must be allowed to pass through it.

You could create a new collision Object Type for the player, but this makes things more difficult for the game project overall. It makes the player-controlled Character different from other Characters in the game, and lots of collision interactions treat the player and enemies the same. This would require a considerable amount of time and effort changing a large number of assets in the game to accommodate for the new collision Object Type.

If instead you create a new collision Object Type called PlayerOnly and assign it to the collision volume, you now have a collision Object Type that the player-controlled Character can respond to (and other Characters in the game can respond to it differently). Then, a new collision preset can be made for the blocking volume, set to block the Pawn collision Object Type, and ignore all other types. And the player-controlled Character's capsule can block the PlayerOnly channel.

So the steps to implement this are:

1. Create a new PlayerOnly collision Object Channel.
    a. Set its default response to Ignore. This will ensure that all current Collision Presets as well as

new future presets will ignore this channel.

2. Set the player-controlled Character's collision preset to block the PlayerOnly channel. If the Capsule Component uses a built-in preset (Pawn, for instance), it can be changed in Project Settings.

3. Add a new collision preset for the blocking volume, called BlockPlayerOnly.

    a. Set its collision Object Type to PlayerOnly.

    b. Set its Collision Enabled to Query Only.

    c. Set it to ignore all collision channels except for Pawn (or whichever Object Type is used by the player-controlled Character's capsule).

Only the player-controlled Character will have a Block interaction with this volume. All other Actors will have an Ignore interaction.

Note that you may need to restart the Unreal Engine editor before you can see the new custom collision preset in the dropdown for components.

While this solution did require an additional collision Object Type, this new Object Type is versatile and can be used in many situations. An example would be player-only overlap volumes.

Example Custom Preset: OverlapPlayerOnly

Trigger volumes are volumes that trigger a response when

overlapped. Most trigger volumes in games only need to respond to the player-controlled Character. There are exceptions, of course, such as bombs and traps that the player can set to damage enemies in the game, but we'll consider player-only trigger volumes for now.

The naïve approach to this is to create a new Actor (a door, floor switch, etc.) and add a Shape Component (such as a Sphere Component, Box Component, etc.).

Let's say we create a new Actor Blueprint called BP_TriggerVolume and add a Sphere Component to it. By default, the Sphere Component's Collision Presets is set to OverlapAllDynamic (at least at the time of writing, during which the latest engine version is 5.4.1). This preset overlaps with all other collision Object Types.

So, your typical solution you might see in a YouTube tutorial might be to bind an overlap callback to **On Component Begin Overlap** on this Sphere Component, then access the **Other Actor** in the callback and cast it to a particular class (your player-controlled Character class, etc.). In general, if you're performing additional filtering after the collision interaction has occurred (such as the casting performed in this example), you may first want to consider a way to filter at the broader phase of collision interactions.

Since this trigger volume should only interact with the player, we can create a new collision preset for it.

1. Create a new collision preset called OverlapPlayerOnly.
    a. Set its Object Type to PlayerOnly.
    b. Set its Collision Enabled to Query Only.
    c. Set its collision response to Pawn to Overlap.
    d. Set its responses to all other channels to Ignore.
2. Set the Sphere Component's Collision Presets to OverlapOnlyPlayer.

Because the Pawn collision Object Type has its response to PlayerOnly set to Block, and the OverlapOnlyPlayer preset has its response to Pawn set to Overlap, the least-blocking interaction between these two is Overlap.

Now we have a collision preset that can be used for any component that needs to register overlap interactions with the player-controlled Character and nothing else. In games with lots of moving Actors, this will have a considerable impact on the game's performance for the better.

Collision Presets are an amazing tool and are criminally underused. Make a habit of using them.

Aside from making the collision interactions in the game more structured, Collision Presets have another strength. They can be used to filter queries. We'll learn more about queries next.

7 – QUERIES – LINE TRACES

Queries are some of the most important tools in game development. Similarly to how we can move objects with collision throughout the world and dictate their collision interactions with their collision profiles, we can also perform queries to probe the world for information. Queries, like objects with collision data, have their own collision properties that determine the results they will obtain when performed.

Three prominent types of queries in Unreal Engine are:

- Line traces
- Shape traces
- Overlap queries

There are variations of each type of query, including:

- Single
- Multi
- Test

And traces can be performed:

- By channel
- By Object Type
- By collision profile

This results in many query utilities based on the various permutations of the above qualities.

Collision query functions perform a query by testing the

geometry of the surrounding environment. This can be done by shooting a ray out into space (line traces), sweeping a shape across space (shape traces), or checking to see if anything overlaps with a given shape (overlap queries).

Much like objects with collision, query functions have their own collision channels. While trace channels are designed to be used for queries, queries can use the object channels as well. The only difference between trace channels and object channels is that trace channels cannot be assigned to objects (Primitive Components).

Perhaps the best way to demonstrate how query functions work is with an example. One of the most common types of query functions is the line trace.

Line Traces - Single

The single line trace by channel is your basic ray cast. The function exists on the UWorld class as LineTraceSingleByChannel and is exposed to Blueprint via the static BlueprintCallable function LineTraceSingle in the Blueprint Function Library UKismetSystemLibrary.

Much like a moving object in a Level, LineTraceSingleByChannel has its own collision channel. The ray is extended into space determined by a start and end location in world space. The trace looks for objects that are configured to block the trace's collision channel. Results of *the first trace hit* are stored in an FHitResult struct, including the hit Actor, Impact Point, Impact Normal, etc. The function itself returns a Boolean reporting the success or failure of the trace (a blocking hit results in a success, and the absence of a blocking hit results in a failure). The function's signature is as follows:

```
bool LineTraceSingleByChannel(
    struct FHitResult& OutHit,
    const FVector& Start,
    const FVector& End,
    ECollisionChannel TraceChannel,
    const FCollisionQueryParams& Params =
FCollisionQueryParams::DefaultQueryParam,
    const FCollisionResponseParams& ResponseParam =
FCollisionResponseParams::DefaultResponseParam)
const;
```

The Hit Result is passed in by non-const reference and is an out parameter as is customary in Unreal Engine code (take your gripes with that to Reddit). This means that the FHitResult argument is passed in by reference (it is not copied) and can be altered from within the function (and that's what happens).

The Start and End parameters are world-space vector locations that determine the trace's start and end, respectively.

TraceChannel is the collision channel for the trace. Objects must be configured to block this channel to register a hit by this trace.

ResponseParam is a commonly overlooked input for this function and is often omitted. What most developers don't know about traces is that they have their own collision responses to the collision channels, much like objects do. By default, a trace's responses to all of the collision channels is Block. These responses can be customized, however. The ResponseParam input parameter is a struct of type FCollisionResponseParams and can hold the collision responses that the trace will have against the collision channels.

Remember the example in Chapter 6 where we created a custom trace channel called FootIK and had the Skeletal Mesh Components on Characters ignore it? This solution requires that Skeletal Mesh Components on Characters ignore the FootIK trace channel. A more elegant solution would be to simply perform a trace that has its collision response to Pawn set to Ignore. This fixes the problem without requiring the collision settings on the Skeletal Mesh Components in the game to be changed. The only drawback to this solution is that the Control Rig graph only has access to exposed trace functions that don't allow for customization of collision responses, so the trace would need to be performed in C++ on another class and fed into the Control Rig, via the Anim Instance, for example.

An example is in order. We'll perform a single line trace by channel first in C++ before examining a Blueprint example.

LineTraceSingleByChannel

We'll perform a single line trace by channel in the `BeginPlay` function on our Character.

```cpp
FHitResult OutHit;
const FVector Start = GetActorLocation();
const FVector End = Start + 500.f *
GetActorForwardVector();
ECollisionChannel CollisionChannel = ECC_Visibility;
FCollisionQueryParams Params;
TArray<AActor*> IgnoredActors;
IgnoredActors.Add(this);
Params.AddIgnoredActors(IgnoredActors);
FCollisionResponseParams ResponseParams;
ResponseParams.CollisionResponse.SetAllChannels(ECR_
Ignore);
ResponseParams.CollisionResponse.SetResponse(ECC_Wor
ldStatic, ECR_Block);

const bool bHit = GetWorld()-
>LineTraceSingleByChannel(
    OutHit,
    Start,
    End,
    CollisionChannel,
    Params,
    ResponseParams);


if (bHit)
{
    DrawDebugSphere(
    GetWorld(),
    OutHit.Location,
    20.f,
    12,
    FColor::Red,
    true,
    60.f);
```

```
}
```

We are tracing from the Character's location outward in its forward direction by 500 units.

The trace has the collision channel Visibility. This means that objects must block the Visibility channel to be detected by this trace.

Note

Most trace examples in this book will use the Visibility channel. Remember that serious projects may often assign custom channels to their traces.

An array of Actors is constructed and the Character itself (this) is added to it before it is added to the collision query params struct Params via AddIgnoredActors. You probably guessed that any Actors in this array will be ignored by the trace, and if you did, you were right.

ResponseParams is created and its CollisionResponse member is accessed to set the collision responses for this trace. The trace's responses to all channels are set to Ignore, then the response to the WorldStatic channel is set to Block. This allows us to filter out any objects that use collision channels other than WorldStatic.

To verify that our trace registers a hit that we expect, a debug sphere is drawn at the trace hit's location.

To test this trace, we can place two objects in front of our Character's starting location in the Level. The first will be a Static Mesh Actor with its Static Mesh Component's collision Object Type set to PhysicsBody. The second will be a Static Mesh Actor with its Static Mesh Component's collision Object Type set to WorldStatic.

Figure 7.1 - The Player Start and Two Static Mesh Actors

Play testing shows that the debug sphere is drawn at the surface of the second Static Mesh Actor—the one whose collision Object Type is WorldStatic. The Actor whose collision Object Type is PhysicsBody is ignored.

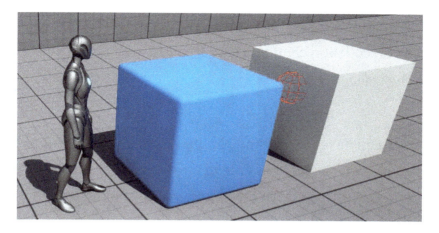

Figure 7.2 – Drawing the Debug Sphere at the Trace Hit Location

We can customize the trace to ignore WorldStatic and block PhysicsBody instead by changing the `ResponseParams` that we pass into the line trace function. All we would need to do is to set the `ResponseParams.CollisionResponse` response to `ECC_PhysicsBody` to `ECR_Block`. I leave this as an exercise for the reader.

Points of Confusion

It's important to consider some points of confusion regarding performing a trace on a collision channel.

The trace's channel belongs to the trace, not hit objects.

This can trip up some developers. Say the channel for the line trace is chosen to be Pawn. This means that the trace will register hits with objects that are set to block the Pawn channel. This does not mean that the trace will register hits with objects whose collision Object Type is Pawn. If an object has its collision Object Type set to Pawn, but has its response to the Pawn collision channel set to Ignore, it will not register a hit for the trace.

Queries can have object collision channels

A trace can have its collision channel set to one of the object channels. This is only possible in C++; the Blueprint-exposed line trace utility function only allows trace channels to be selected. Tracing using trace channels makes intuitive sense. It's important to understand that to trace with an object channel is not tracing to hit objects using that object type, but rather is tracing to hit objects that *block* that object type.

Traces block all collision channels by default

A trace has its default responses to all channels set to Block by default. It is only because we passed in a customized ResponseParams struct to `LineTraceSingleByChannel` in the above example that our trace ignored all collision channels except the one we specified via calls to `SetAllChannels` and `SetResponse` on the ResponseParams's `CollisionResponse` member. Line traces performed in Blueprint do not have the capability to customize their responses.

Line Trace By Channel

In Blueprint, the exposed utility for a single line trace by channel is the **Line Trace By Channel** function on Kismet System Library.

While it lacks the ability to customize its collision responses as is possible in C++, it does come with the ability to draw a debug line and point for the trace via the dropdown titled **Draw Debug Type**.

This function only gives the option to choose a trace channel for its collision channel. Object channels cannot be chosen.

A Boolean is provided for the option to trace against complex geometry. This is of course more expensive and used less often.

The following figure shows an example usage of **Line Trace By Channel** on **Begin Play** for the project's Character. The trace is performed from the Character's location outward in its forward direction by 500 units. The trace uses the Visibility channel and has the Character itself added to an array passed into **Actors to Ignore**.

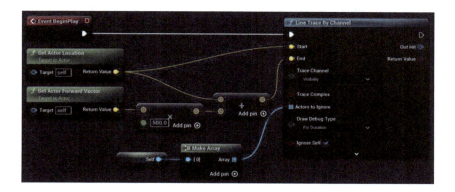

Figure 7.3 – Line Trace By Channel

The following figure shows the debug line and point produced by this trace upon hitting an object that is set to block the Visibility channel. The line is red up until it reaches a collision, at which point it turns green for the remainder of the length of the trace.

Figure 7.4 – Debug Line and Point for the Trace

The Static Mesh Actor in front of the Character has its collision response to Visibility set to Block in Figure 7.4. Changing its response to Overlap or Ignore will result in the trace failing to register a hit on the mesh.

Tips

Consider the following tips when working with line traces.

Don't call the Blueprint interface from C++

The **Line Trace By Channel** Blueprint function is exposed from the KistmetSystemLibrary.h file. The native C++ function name for it is LineTraceSingle. It is a static C++ function and there is nothing stopping you from calling it from C++. However, there are already enough line trace functions built-into the engine, and this just adds another one into the mix. Use the LineTraceSingleByChannel function on UWorld in C++ (it affords you more options anyway, as we've seen in the above example).

Use DrawDebugLineTraceSingle to Debug

In the above example, we drew a debug sphere at the trace hit location. If you want the same debug capabilities as the Blueprint-exposed line trace function, mimic its implementation by calling `DrawDebugLineTraceSingle`, which draws a line for the trace and a point for the hit, as well as allows for custom colors for the trace and hit. We'll use this function in our next example.

The single line trace by channel is flexible and versatile, but it's not the only type of line trace.

LineTraceSingleByProfile

Line traces can trace according to a profile, rather than a collision channel.

What this means is that you can assign a collision profile to the trace, and the trace will have the Object Type and Collision Responses of that profile.

For instance, say you wish to perform a line trace with the WorldStatic collision Object Type and Block responses to all collision channels. You could trace using the BlockAll collision profile, since it has the WorldStatic collision Object Type and Block responses to all channels. Any object that blocks the WorldStatic collision channel will register a hit for this line trace.

`LineTraceSingleByProfile` behaves the same way as `LineTraceSingleByChannel`. The only difference is the way the trace's collision channel and responses are configured. With `LineTraceSingleByChannel`, the channel is explicitly set via an input argument to the function, and the responses are set in the Response Params. In `LineTraceSingleByProfile`, the trace's collision channel and responses are dictated by the collision profile chosen.

In the following example, we are performing a single line trace by profile in the Character's `BeginPlay` function and using `DrawDebugLineTraceSingle` to showcase the result.

```
FHitResult OutHit;
const FVector Start = GetActorLocation();
const FVector End = Start + 500.f *
GetActorForwardVector();
FCollisionQueryParams Params;
TArray<AActor*> IgnoredActors;
IgnoredActors.Add(this);
Params.AddIgnoredActors(IgnoredActors);

const bool bHit = GetWorld()-
>LineTraceSingleByProfile(
    OutHit,
    Start,
    End,
    FName("BlockAll"),
    Params);

DrawDebugLineTraceSingle(
    GetWorld(),
    Start,
    End,
    EDrawDebugTrace::ForDuration,
    bHit,
    OutHit,
    FLinearColor::Red,
```

```
FLinearColor::Green,
30.f);
```

We start the line trace at the Character's own location and end it 500 units outward in the Character's forward direction. We construct an array of Actors and add the Character itself (this) to it, then add it to the Params with AddIgnoredActors.

The collision profile is chosen by name, passing in an FName to LineTraceSingleByProfile. "BlockAll" is chosen as the collision profile name. The above code block also demonstrates how to make a call to DrawDebugLineTraceSingle to show the results of the trace.

Line Trace By Profile

The Blueprint version of LineTraceSingleByProfile is **Line Trace By Profile.**

The collision profile name is a Name input parameter for the node. It also has a dropdown containing the collision profile names in the project. The other input parameters are the same as those in **Line Trace By Channel.**

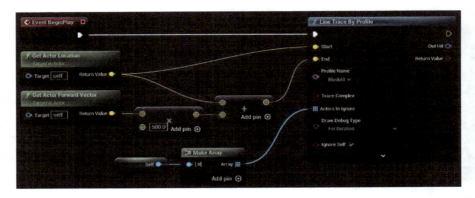

Figure 7.5 – Line Trace By Profile

The call to **Line Trace By Profile** in the figure above shows the same trace as the C++ example of `LineTraceSingleByProfile`.

Tips

Keep the following in mind when using single line traces by profile.

Tracing by profile doesn't look for objects using the chosen profile. While it may sound like "**Line Trace By Profile**" looks for objects using the chosen profile, this isn't the case. The trace behaves the same as **Line Trace By Channel**. The only difference is that we are setting the trace's channel and responses via a collision profile.

Tracing by profile is a good way to filter the collision interactions of traces, as is tracing by channel. By this point, I hope you understand that the objects hit by the trace register hits based on their responses to the trace's channel. Their object types are not what determines whether they register a hit.

If you want to trace objects based on their collision Object Type, you need to use line traces by object type.

LineTraceSingleByObjectType

While `LineTraceSingleByProfile` works the same way as `LineTraceSingleByChannel`, `LineTraceSingleByObjectType` works differently.

The first two types of traces—by channel and by Object Type—take advantage of collision filtering. If a component's collision profile is not configured to have a Block interaction with the trace's profile, it will not register a hit. Tracing by Object Type however does not use collision filtering. Objects that use the specified Object Type register hits regardless of their Collision Responses. In fact, an object can have its responses to all channels set to Ignore and still register a hit by this trace! The only requirement is that the object be configured to use queries (via its Collision Enabled setting).

The following code snippet shows an example of how to perform a trace by Object Type in the Character's `BeginPlay` function:

```cpp
FHitResult OutHit;
const FVector Start = GetActorLocation();
const FVector End = Start + 500.f *
```

```cpp
GetActorForwardVector();
FCollisionQueryParams Params;
TArray<AActor*> IgnoredActors;
IgnoredActors.Add(this);
Params.AddIgnoredActors(IgnoredActors);
FCollisionObjectQueryParams ObjectQueryParams;
ObjectQueryParams.AddObjectTypesToQuery(ECC_WorldDyn
amic);
ObjectQueryParams.AddObjectTypesToQuery(ECC_WorldSta
tic);

const bool bHit = GetWorld()-
>LineTraceSingleByObjectType(
    OutHit,
    Start,
    End,
    ObjectQueryParams,
    Params);

DrawDebugLineTraceSingle(
    GetWorld(),
    Start,
    End,
    EDrawDebugTrace::ForDuration,
    bHit,
    OutHit,
    FLinearColor::Red,
    FLinearColor::Green,
    30.f);
```

Notice that multiple collision channels can be added to the Collision Object Query Params.

Unreal Engine's collision framework is powerful because of its collision filtering capabilities. Tracing for Object Types bypasses collision filtering altogether and simply queries by collision Object Type alone.

Because a project doesn't (and shouldn't) have many collision channels, performing a query by Object Type will result in a potentially large number of possible hits. This in turn may require additional filtering after the hits are registered (such as by casting). Think twice before performing a trace by Object Type. Would it be better to filter the collision by taking advantage of Collision Responses?

Line Trace For Objects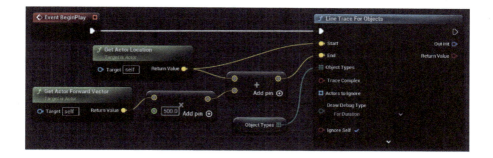

Line Trace For Objects is the Blueprint version of LineTraceSingleByObjectType.

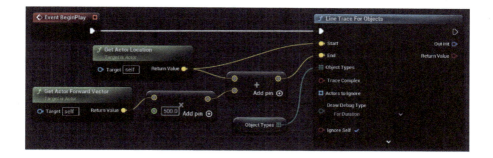

Figure 7.6 – Line Trace For Objects

Note that Object Types is passed in as an array, and that multiple Object Types can be added to the trace.

Line Trace Test Functions

Test versions of each line trace function exist which see if a blocking hit occurs. These functions only return a Boolean value—true if there is a blocking hit, false if otherwise. These are more performant and can be used when additional information about the hit is not needed, such as the hit Actor or Impact Location.

Test versions of the line trace functions include:

- `LineTraceTestByChannel`
- `LineTraceTestByObjectType`
- `LineTraceTestByProfile`

Use these when you merely need to know if a line trace would get a hit, but you don't need any additional data.

Line Traces - Multi

There exist "multi" versions of each type of line trace.

These trace a ray against the world and return all overlaps up to the first blocking hit. The results are stored in an array, each element being an overlap until the last (which is the blocking hit, if found).

Let's see how this works with an example.

LineTraceMultiByChannel

This function takes in an array of Hit Results (by non-const reference, i.e. an "out parameter"). This array will be filled in with registered overlaps and the last blocking hit, if found. The functions take in a start and end, a trace channel, Collision Query Parameters, and Collision Response Parameters, just like `LineTraceSingleByChannel` does.

This function behaves differently than `LineTraceSingleByChannel`, however. All objects which register an Overlap interaction with the trace will be stored in the Hit Result array, up to the blocking hit, if any.

The function returns a Boolean which will be true if the trace contains a blocking hit, and false otherwise.

Let's say your game decides to develop a new type of hit scan weapon. Hit scan weapons use line traces when being fired, scoring an instantaneous hit on the object hit by the line trace. This new type of weapon is designed to shoot through Characters, scoring a hit on each Character that the ray passes through. Walls should block the trace. This is an opportunity to use LineTraceSingleByChannel.

Let's say that Characters in the game have their Skeletal Mesh Components using the collision preset CharacterMesh. You decide that this preset should block the trace channel used by the weapon. In Project Settings -> Engine -> Collision -> Preset, you find CharacterMesh, and select Edit... to change its Collision Responses. The response to the collision channel used by the weapon can be set to Overlap (for this example, we'll use Visibility, but in a serious game project, this might merit its own trace channel, such as Weapon or MultiWeapon).

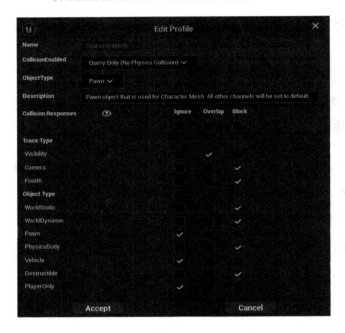

Figure 7.7 —CharacterMesh has an Overlap Response to
Visibility

We can then perform a multi line trace by channel, configuring our trace to ignore all channels except Pawn and WorldStatic (assuming that our Character's Skeletal Mesh Component has the Pawn Object Type and the walls have the WorldStatic Object Type). The trace can block these channels.

Since the CharacterMesh collision profile has an Overlap response to the Visibility channel, the resulting interaction with the trace will be Overlap for the Skeletal Mesh Component on Characters. Walls can have a Block response to the Visibility channel to register a blocking hit for the trace.

The following code shows how to perform this line trace.

```
TArray<FHitResult> OutHits;
const FVector Start = GetActorLocation() +
FVector(0.f, 0.f, 80.f);
const FVector End = Start + 1000.f *
GetActorForwardVector();
FCollisionQueryParams Params;
TArray<AActor*> IgnoredActors;
IgnoredActors.Add(this);
Params.AddIgnoredActors(IgnoredActors);
FCollisionResponseParams ResponseParams;
ResponseParams.CollisionResponse.SetAllChannels(ECR_
Ignore);
ResponseParams.CollisionResponse.SetResponse(ECC_Paw
n, ECR_Block);
ResponseParams.CollisionResponse.SetResponse(ECC_Wor
ldStatic, ECR_Block);

const bool bHit = GetWorld()-
>LineTraceMultiByChannel(
    OutHits,
    Start,
    End,
    ECC_Visibility,
    Params,
    ResponseParams);
```

The line trace is raised by 80 units to simulate a head shot. We trace from the starting location outward in the forward direction by 1000 units. The trace here is performed inside the project's Character class for demonstration purposes (your project would perform this trace in a class suited to handle weapon tracing). The Character itself is added to the IgnoredActors array, which is added to the Query Parameters.

Notice that the trace is configured to ignore all channels except Pawn and WorldStatic. This filters out objects using the other collision channels. The trace is performed on the Visibility channel, though as mentioned previously, a more serious project would likely have a custom trace channel for this trace.

To showcase the results, we can make use of DrawDebugLineTraceMulti, which will draw lines and points to indicate blocking hits.

```
DrawDebugLineTraceMulti(
    GetWorld(),
    Start,
    End,
    EDrawDebugTrace::ForDuration,
    bHit,
    OutHits,
    FLinearColor::Red,
    FLinearColor::Green,
    30.f);
```

We will also loop through the OutHits array to show that the Hit Result's bBlockingHit Boolean will only be true for the blocking hit, despite the Hit Result containing useful information for the non-blocking hits (these are the overlaps). To prove that these non-blocking hits contain useful information, we'll draw debug spheres at their ImpactPoints. Note the use of the ternary operator to choose the radius of the debug sphere as well as its color based on the value of bBlockingHit.

```
for (FHitResult& Hit : OutHits)
{
    DrawDebugSphere(
        GetWorld(),
```

```
        Hit.ImpactPoint,
        Hit.bBlockingHit ? 15.f : 10.f,
        12,
        Hit.bBlockingHit ? FColor::Red :
FColor::White,
        false,
        30.f);
}
```

Performing this trace in `BeginPlay` with three Skeletal Mesh Components in front of the player-controlled Character, we can see that we have registered three overlaps. The wall behind the line of Character meshes shows that a blocking hit was registered. Our debug spheres further confirm these results.

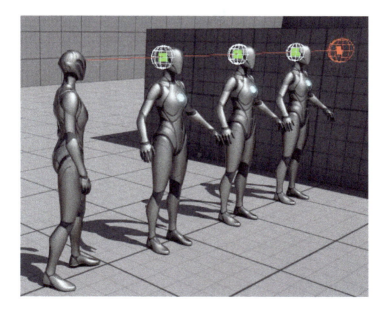

Figure 7.8 – Results of LineTraceMultiByChannel

We can also see that placing a wall between the trace and the target will produce a blocking hit before that target can register an overlap.

Figure 7.9 – Hitting a Blocking Wall

Notice that the trace reaches past the wall and passes through the mesh on the other side. However, because a blocking hit has already been registered by this point, the mesh on the other side of the wall will not register an overlap. The trace will only return all overlaps up to the blocking hit, as well as the blocking hit itself, of course.

This allows for the example weapon to be able to shoot through multiple Characters, yet still be blocked by walls.

Multi Line Trace By Channel

Multi Line Trace By Channel is the Blueprint version of `LineTraceMultiByChannel`. The following shows how to perform the same trace as demonstrated above. Note however that the Blueprint version does not allow for customization of the trace's collision responses. This means that the trace will have a blocking response to all channels, limiting our ability to do collision filtering.

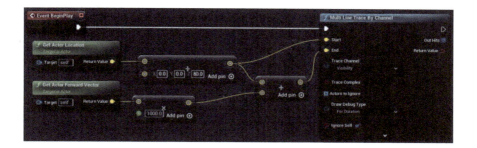

Figure 7.10 – Multi Line Trace by Channel

The following figure shows the results of the trace with an object between the two target meshes. This object (the chamfered block) has an object type of PhysicsBody and an Overlap response to the Visibility channel.

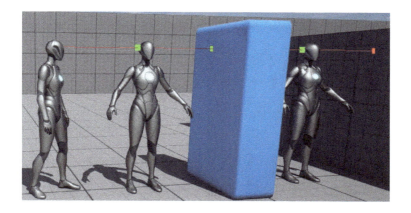

Figure 7.11 – Multi Line Trace in Blueprint

Line traces are one of the cases where there are clear benefits to using C++ for their implementation over Blueprint.

Tips

Keep these tips in mind when performing multi line traces.

Multi line traces register overlaps up to the first blocking hit.
While the trace can register a hit, it doesn't *have to* register a hit. You can utilize a multi-trace merely for the overlap results if that's all you need.

The first blocking hit will prevent the trace from further registering overlaps.
Remember that, as shown in Figure 7.9, placing a blocking object between the two target meshes prevented the trace from reaching the second mesh. A blocking hit will stop the trace in its tracks. Make sure you understand that when implementing a multi-line trace.

Multi Line Traces By Profile and Object Type

Similarly to single line traces, multi-line traces can be performed by profile and by Object Type as well. These traces perform similarly to `LineTraceMultiByChannel`, except for the differences outlined below.

LineTraceMultiByProfile

Like `LineTraceMultiByChannel`, `LineTraceMultiByProfile` registers all overlaps up to a blocking hit, except that the trace channel and responses for the trace are determined by the trace profile, much like `LineTraceSingleByProfile`.

Multi Line Trace By Profile

This is the Blueprint version of `LineTraceMultiByProfile`. It behaves the same as its C++ equivalent.

LineTraceMultiByObjectType

Like `LineTraceMultiByChannel`, this trace registers all overlaps up to a blocking hit, except that it traces for the specified object type, like `LineTraceSingleByObjectType`. Does not take objects' Collision Responses into account.

Multi Line Trace For Objects

The Blueprint equivalent of `LineTraceMultiByObjectType`. The Object Types are passed in as an array.

As you can see, there are many options for line traces. The type of line trace you end up choosing should depend on your needs.

Tips

Keep these tips in mind when performing line traces.

Don't use two traces when one will do.

If you find yourself performing multiple traces, ask yourself if you can achieve the same results with a single trace. You don't need to perform multiple line traces to shoot a ray through multiple objects—use a multi-line trace for that.

Avoid filtering results after the trace.

If you find yourself filtering trace results manually, such as by casting, ask yourself if you can filter the traces at the broader phase of collision filtering via Collision Responses, both for objects' collision profiles and for the trace itself.

If you understand the various flavors of line traces in Unreal Engine, you are equipped to understand the suite of shape sweeps, as they behave similarly.

9 – QUERIES – SHAPE SWEEPS

While traces shoot a ray out into space to detect hits (in the case of single line traces) and overlaps (in the case of multi-line traces) shape sweeps shoot a shape out into space instead.

This can be useful for gameplay mechanics that require more leeway. It's not very often that a game requires pinpoint accuracy in all situations. Shooting a hit scan weapon that requires perfect precision can make a game unnecessarily difficult. If instead a hit can be registered when the weapon's trajectory is "close enough," players may have more fun because they are hitting more targets.

Shape sweeps are perfect for determining hits while giving more leeway.

Single Shape Sweeps

In C++, single sweeps can be performed using `SweepSingleByChannel`. This function can be configured for various shapes, i.e. spheres, boxes, capsules, etc. A number of functions are exposed to Blueprint which call this function, configuring it for various shapes.

SweepSingleByChannel

To perform a shape sweep with `SweepSingleByChannel`, we must create and pass in a Collision Shape. A Collision Shape is a struct of type FCollisionShape, a data structure that contains an ECollisionShape enum that can be one of the following:

- Line
- Box
- Sphere
- Capsule

This struct has a number of utilities for setting the shape parameters for the chosen shape, as well as the ability to create the chosen shape via several static factory functions.

You can make a sphere Collision Shape with the static MakeSphere function, which accepts a sphere radius:

```
FCollisionShape Sphere =
FCollisionShape::MakeSphere(50.f);
```

Similarly, there are functions for making the other shapes:

```
FCollisionShape Box =
FCollisionShape::MakeBox(FVector(25.f, 25.f, 25.f));
FCollisionShape Capsule =
FCollisionShape::MakeCapsule(44.f, 88.f);
FCollisionShape Line = FCollisionShape::LineShape;
```

Notice that LineShape requires no dimensions. MakeBox accepts a 3-dimensional vector for the half-extent, and MakeCapsule accepts a capsule radius and half-height.

Performing a Sphere Sweep by Channel

We can set up the sphere sweep with a Hit Result, start and end locations, Collision Query Params, and Collision Response Params just as we can with line traces.

```
FHitResult OutHit;
const FVector Start = GetActorLocation() +
FVector(0.f, 0.f, 80.f);
const FVector End = Start + 500.f *
GetActorForwardVector();
FCollisionQueryParams Params;
TArray<AActor*> IgnoredActors;
IgnoredActors.Add(this);
Params.AddIgnoredActors(IgnoredActors);
FCollisionResponseParams ResponseParams;
ResponseParams.CollisionResponse.SetAllChannels(ECR_
Ignore);
ResponseParams.CollisionResponse.SetResponse(ECC_Paw
n, ECR_Block);
ResponseParams.CollisionResponse.SetResponse(ECC_Wor
ldStatic, ECR_Block);
```

We can then set up the Collision Shape and call SweepSingleByChannel.

```
const float SphereRadius = 12.f;
FCollisionShape Sphere =
FCollisionShape::MakeSphere(SphereRadius);

bool const bHit = GetWorld()->SweepSingleByChannel(
    OutHit,
    Start,
    End,
    FQuat::Identity,
    ECC_Visibility,
    Sphere,
    Params,
    ResponseParams);
```

The only unfamiliar parameter you should notice is the FQuat. Shapes can be swept with a rotation, and this rotation is passed in in the form of a quaternion. If you have a desired rotation in the form of an FRotator, simply convert it to an FQuat either via the FRotator::Quaternion function, or the static FQuat::MakeFromRotator function. Both methods are outlined below.

```
FRotator Rotation;
FQuat Quat = Rotation.Quaternion();
FQuat Quat2 = FQuat::MakeFromRotator(Rotation);
```

We can draw a debug for the trace with DrawDebugSphereTraceSingle:

```
DrawDebugSphereTraceSingle(GetWorld(),
    Start,
    End,
    SphereRadius,
    EDrawDebugTrace::ForDuration,
    bHit,
    OutHit,
    FLinearColor::Red,
    FLinearColor::Green,
    30.f);
```

This allows us to see the results of the sphere trace while testing the game. The following figure shows the results of the sphere trace. Notice that the target mesh is positioned slightly to the right, and that a normal line trace would have missed it. A sphere trace gave enough leeway to allow for a hit even with a less-than-perfect aim.

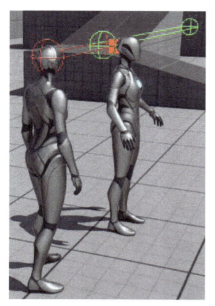

Figure 9.1 – Performing a Sphere Trace

Here, the target mesh has the collision Object Type Pawn, and is configured to Block the Visibility channel.

Sphere Trace By Channel

Kismet System Library exposes a BlueprintCallable function that performs this same type of trace, called **Sphere Trace By Channel**. We get the same results with the following call to this function in Blueprint. Again, keep in mind that in Blueprint, we do not have the ability to customize the trace responses as we do in C++ with Collision Response Params.

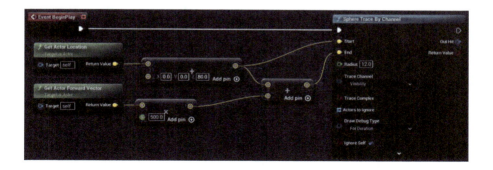

Figure 9.2 – Performing a Sphere Trace in Blueprint

Performing a box trace or capsule trace in C++ is as simple as changing the collision to a box or capsule. There are draw debug functions for these other shapes as well.

Box Trace By Channel

Box Trace By Channel is the Blueprint-exposed function for performing a box trace. Its native C++ function name is `BoxTraceSingle`, and the function simply calls `SweepSingleByChannel` passing in a box Collision Shape via the `FCollisionShape::MakeBox` static function.

Capsule Trace By Channel

Capsule Trace By Channel is the Blueprint-exposed function for performing a capsule trace. Its native C++ function name is `CapsuleTraceSingle`, and the function simply calls `SweepSingleByChannel` passing in a capsule Collision Shape via the `FCollisionShape::MakeCapsule` static function.

Multi Shape Sweeps By Channel

Shape sweeps by channel can be multi, just as line traces can. The `UWorld` class has a `SweepMultiByChannel` function that can be configured to sweep with the same selection of shapes we've seen for the single shape sweep.

SweepMultiByChannel

We can perform a multi box trace by first preparing our parameters. Remember that for multi-traces, we needed an array of Hit Results. We will likewise need an array of Hit Results for a multi-sweep.

```
TArray<FHitResult> OutHits;
const FVector Start = GetActorLocation() +
FVector(0.f, 0.f, 80.f);
const FVector End = Start + 500.f *
GetActorForwardVector();
FCollisionQueryParams Params;
TArray<AActor*> IgnoredActors;
IgnoredActors.Add(this);
Params.AddIgnoredActors(IgnoredActors);
FCollisionResponseParams ResponseParams;
ResponseParams.CollisionResponse.SetAllChannels(ECR_
Ignore);
ResponseParams.CollisionResponse.SetResponse(ECC_Paw
n, ECR_Block);
ResponseParams.CollisionResponse.SetResponse(ECC_Wor
ldStatic, ECR_Block);
```

We must also prepare a Collision Shape. We will create a box
Collision Shape, specifying the half-extent (it will be longer in
its local Z direction). We will also specify a rotation for the box
with a Rotator.

```
const FVector BoxHalfExtent(25.f, 25.f, 45.f);
FCollisionShape Box =
FCollisionShape::MakeBox(BoxHalfExtent);
const FRotator BoxRotation(45.f, 45.f, 45.f);
```

Next, we can perform the multi-trace with
SweepMultiByChannel.

```
bool const bHit = GetWorld()->SweepMultiByChannel(
    OutHits,
    Start,
    End,
    BoxRotation.Quaternion(),
    ECC_Visibility,
    Box,
    Params,
```

```
ResponseParams);
```

We can draw a debug for the sweep with
DrawDebugBoxTraceMulti.

```
DrawDebugBoxTraceMulti(
    GetWorld(),
    Start,
    End,
    BoxHalfExtent,
    BoxRotation,
    EDrawDebugTrace::ForDuration,
    bHit,
    OutHits,
    FLinearColor::Red,
    FLinearColor::Green,
    30.f);
```

The following figure shows the results of the box trace. Each
Quinn mesh has the collision Object Type Pawn and is
configured to Overlap the Visibility channel.

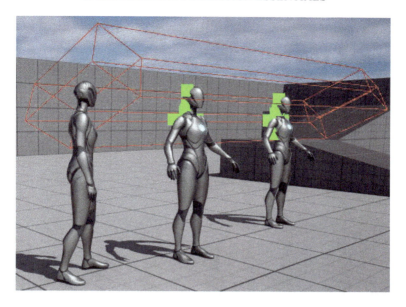

Figure 9.3 – Results of a Multi Box Sweep

Notice that we had multiple overlaps per mesh. Multi shape sweeps will detect overlaps with each Physics Body on a Skeletal Mesh Component's Physics Asset. We can print the names of the bones corresponding to each Physics Body hit by looping over the Hit Results and accessing the bone name for each hit:

```
for (FHitResult& Hit : OutHits)
{
    FString BoneNameString;
    Hit.BoneName.ToString(BoneNameString);
    FString Message =
FString::Format(TEXT("Overlapped with: {0}"),
{BoneNameString});

    GEngine->AddOnScreenDebugMessage(
    -1,
    30.f,
    FColor::Red,
    Message);
}
```

There are Blueprint-exposed functions for performing multi-shape sweeps as well.

Multi Box Trace By Channel

The following nodes will perform a multi-box sweep:

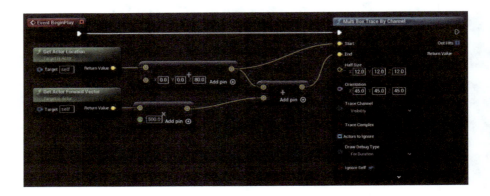

Figure 9.4 – Multi Box Trace By Channel

And the results are shown below:

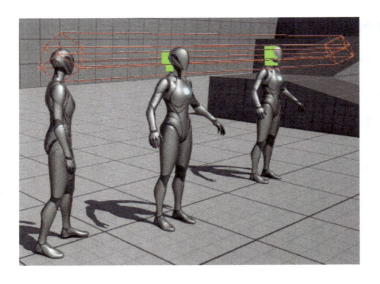

Figure 9.5 – Results of a Multi Box Trace

Similar functions are exposed to Blueprint for sphere and capsule shapes.

Multi Sphere Trace By Channel

This is the `BlueprintCallable` function with the native C++ name `SphereTraceMulti`. It calls `SweepMultiByChannel`, drawing a debug for the trace with `DrawDebugSphereTraceMulti`.

Multi Capsule Trace By Channel

This is the `BlueprintCallable` function with the native C++ name `CapsuleTraceMulti`. It calls `SweepMultiByChannel`, drawing a debug for the trace with `DrawDebugCapsuleTraceMulti`.

Shape Sweep Function Variations

There are variations of shape sweep functions for sweeping by collision profile and collision Object Type as well.

SweepSingleByProfile

Performs a single shape sweep, just like `SweepSingleByChannel`. The difference is that `SweepSingleByProfile` uses a collision profile to determine the sweep's collision channel and responses.

SweepSingleByObjectType

Performs a single shape sweep. Does not use collision filtering. The sweep is performed against objects of the specified collision Object Type, regardless of their Collision Responses.

SweepMultiByProfile

Performs a multi shape sweep, just like SweepMultiByChannel. The difference is that SweepSingleByProfile uses a collision profile to determine the sweep's collision channel and responses, whereas SweepMultiByChannel specifies a collision channel via an input parameter. Will return multiple overlaps with the same Skeletal Mesh Component if multiple Physics Bodies are overlapped on the Physics Asset.

SweepMultiByObjectType

Performs a multi shape sweep. Does not use collision filtering. The sweep is performed against objects of the specified collision Object Type, regardless of their Collision Responses. Will return multiple overlaps with the same Skeletal Mesh Component if multiple Physics Bodies are overlapped on the Physics Asset.

Multi Box Trace By Profile

This is the BlueprintCallable function with the native C++ name BoxTraceMultiByProfile. It calls

122

SweepMultiByProfile, drawing a debug for the trace with DrawDebugBoxTraceMulti.

Multi Box Trace For Objects

This is the BlueprintCallable function with the native C++ name BoxTraceMultiForObjects. It calls SweepMultiByObjectType, drawing a debug for the trace with DrawDebugBoxTraceMulti.

Multi Sphere Trace By Profile

This is the BlueprintCallable function with the native C++ name SphereTraceMultiByProfile. It calls SweepMultiByProfile, drawing a debug for the trace with DrawDebugSphereTraceMulti.

Multi Sphere Trace For Objects

This is the BlueprintCallable function with the native C++ name SphereTraceMultiForObjects. It calls SweepMultiByObjectType, drawing a debug for the trace with DrawDebugSphereTraceMulti.

Multi Capsule Trace By Profile

This is the BlueprintCallable function with the native C++ name CapsuleTraceMultiByProfile. It calls SweepMultiByProfile, drawing a debug for the trace with DrawDebugCapsuleTraceMulti.

Multi Capsule Trace For Objects

This is the `BlueprintCallable` function with the native C++ name `CapsuleTraceMultiForObjects`. It calls `SweepMultiByObjectType`, drawing a debug for the trace with `DrawDebugCapsuleTraceMulti`.

As you can see, there are a large number of shape sweep function variations. Pick the best variation based on the situation.

Tips

Keep these tips in mind when working with multi-sweeps.

Multi-sweeps register multiple overlaps on a Skeletal Mesh Component.

As seen in the above examples, a shape sweep will detect multiple overlaps on a Skeletal Mesh Component. This is because each individual Physics Body on the Physics Asset registers a separate overlap.

Use the C++ versions to customize the Collision Responses for the sweep.

As you cannot customize collision responses for the sweep using the Blueprint-exposed versions, sweeps will be less optimized, triggering overlaps with all objects configured to block or overlap the sweep. Filter hits and overlaps out at the broader phase of collision filtering rather than after the trace, such as by casting.

These are not the only sweep functions available. The reader is encouraged to peruse the World.h header file to see the other variations, such as the component sweeps (sweeps that use the geometry of a supplied component rather than one of the previously demonstrated basic shapes).

10 – QUERIES – OVERLAP TESTS

I often see developers perform a shape sweep for which the start and end locations are the same—in other words, a sweep of zero length. In these cases, all that is needed is to see if there is an overlap with a specified shape in a specified location. This does not require a sweep at all, but rather an overlap test.

These functions return arrays of Overlap Results, which contain information about the overlap as well as a Boolean, bBlockingHit, that is true if the collision interaction was a blocking one.

OverlapMultiByChannel

The OverlapMultiByChannel function performs an overlap test using the supplied geometrical shape parameters and produces an array of Overlap Result structs. We can prepare the parameters as follows.

```
TArray<struct FOverlapResult> OverlapResults;
const float SphereRadius = 200.f;
FCollisionShape Sphere =
FCollisionShape::MakeSphere(SphereRadius);
FCollisionQueryParams Params;
TArray<AActor*> IgnoredActors;
IgnoredActors.Add(this);
Params.AddIgnoredActors(IgnoredActors);
FCollisionResponseParams ResponseParams;
ResponseParams.CollisionResponse.SetAllChannels(ECR_
Ignore);
ResponseParams.CollisionResponse.SetResponse(ECC_Paw
```

```
n, ECR_Block);
```

We create a sphere Collision Shape with a radius of 200. We also create Collision Query Params and add an array with the Character (this) to the ignored Actors. We create Collision Response Params and customize the Collision Responses for the overlap test.

We can perform the overlap test as follows:

```
const bool bHits = GetWorld()-
>OverlapMultiByChannel(
    OverlapResults,
    GetActorLocation(),
    FQuat::Identity,
    ECC_Visibility,
    Sphere,
    Params,
    ResponseParams);
```

The Boolean returned by this function will be true if there are registered overlaps. We pass in the Overlap Result array by non-const reference so the function can fill it in. To visualize the overlap test, we can draw a sphere with the same radius and position as the overlap test. We will also see if the overlapped component is a Skinned Mesh Component, because if so, we can draw spheres at the locations of each Physics Body in the Physics Asset. This way, we can demonstrate how the overlap query registers multiple overlaps, much like multi-sweeps do.

```
for (FOverlapResult& Overlap : OverlapResults)
{
    USkinnedMeshComponent* MeshComp =
Cast<USkinnedMeshComponent>(Overlap.Component);
    if (IsValid(MeshComp))
    {
        DrawDebugSphere(
        GetWorld(),
        MeshComp-
>GetBoneLocation(Overlap.PhysicsObject-
>GetBodyName()),
        3.f,
        8,
        FColor::Cyan,
        true,
        30.f,
        -1);
    }
}
DrawDebugSphere(
    GetWorld(),
    GetActorLocation(),
    SphereRadius,
    24,
    FColor::Red,
    true,
    -1);
```

The following figure shows the results of an overlap test registering overlaps a Skeletal Mesh Component.

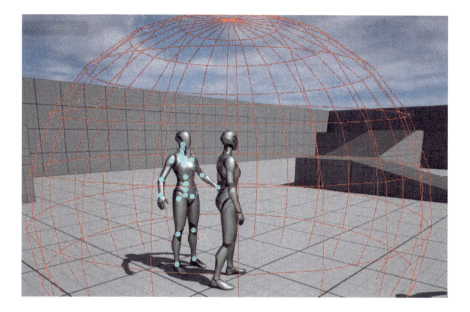

Figure 10.1 – Results from an Overlap Query

A value of -1 was used for the depth priority of the debug spheres drawn at each Physics Body location in the Skeletal Mesh Component so that we could see them through the mesh.

There exist similar functions for performing overlap tests by collision profile and collision Object Type as well.

OverlapMultiByProfile

This function behaves similarly to OverlapMultiByChannel, except that its collision channel and responses are determined by the chosen collision profile.

OverlapMultiByObjectType

This function registers overlaps based on collision Object Type alone. It does not make use of collision filtering.

Tips

Keep these tips in mind when working with overlap queries.

Physics Bodies register overlaps and hits.

Each Physics Body on the Physics Asset will register an overlap or hit, which may or may not be what you want. If you need an overlap or hit for each Physics Body, and perhaps need to use the location of that Physics Body, you can. If you simply need to register an overlap or hit for the Actor itself, consider filtering out the Skeletal Mesh Component and query for the Capsule Component instead.

Filter out Characters if you're not querying for them.

Newer developers often configure their overlap queries and traces to hit everything. Not taking advantage of collision filtering is one of the quickest ways to impact your game's performance. If tracing or querying for objects other than the Characters in the game, filter them out at the broader phase of collision filtering, rather than manually after registering overlaps and hits, such as by casting. Registering a hit for every single Physics Body on every single Character adds up quickly.

Kismet System Library exposes `BlueprintCallable` functions for performing overlap tests using specific shapes.

Sphere Overlap Components

This is the Blueprint-exposed function with the native C++

UNREAL ENGINE 5 COLLISION ESSENTIALS

name `SphereOverlapComponents`. The function calls `OverlapMultiByObjectType`, performing an overlap test by collision Object Type, making no use of collision filtering. This function queries for overlapping components, producing an array of Primitive Components that registered overlaps. The function receives an array of collision Object Types. It also receives an **Actor Class Filter**, a `UClass` pointer that allows for filtering by class, as well as a standard array of **Actors to Ignore**.

Sphere Overlap Actors

This is the Blueprint-exposed function with the native C++ name `SphereOverlapActors`. This function actually just calls `SphereOverlapComponents`, retrieving the array of overlapped components and producing an array of the components' owning Actors. It does this by calling `GetActorListFromComponentList`.

`GetActorListFromComponentList` accepts an array of Primitive Components, loops over them, finds their owners, then adds them uniquely (no duplicates) to an array of Actors.

This results in querying and registering a potentially large number of components, only to cull out their owners in a single array.

Box Overlap Components

This is the Blueprint-exposed function with the native C++ name `BoxOverlapComponents`. The function calls `OverlapMultiByObjectType`, performing an overlap test by collision Object Type, making no use of collision filtering. This function queries for overlapping components, producing an array of Primitive Components that registered overlaps. The function receives an array of collision Object Types. It also receives an **Actor Class Filter**, a `UClass` pointer that allows for filtering by class, as well as a standard array of **Actors to Ignore**.

Box Overlap Actors

This is the Blueprint-exposed function with the native C++ name `BoxOverlapActors`. This function actually just calls `BoxOverlapComponents`, retrieving the array of overlapped components and producing an array of the components' owning Actors. It does this by calling `GetActorListFromComponentList`.

Capsule Overlap Components

This is the Blueprint-exposed function with the native C++ name `CapsuleOverlapComponents`. The function calls `OverlapMultiByObjectType`, performing an overlap test by collision Object Type, making no use of collision filtering. This function queries for overlapping components, producing an array of Primitive Components that registered overlaps. The function receives an array of collision Object Types. It also receives an Actor Class Filter, a UClass pointer that allows for filtering by class, as well as a standard array of Actors to Ignore.

Capsule Overlap Actors

This is the Blueprint-exposed function with the native C++ name CapsuleOverlapActors. This function actually just calls CapsuleOverlapComponents, retrieving the array of overlapped components and producing an array of the components' owning Actors. It does this by calling GetActorListFromComponentList.

More Overlap Tests

While this chapter covers many of the types of overlap queries built-into Unreal Engine, there are still more. ComponentOverlapMulti and ComponentOverlapMultiByChannel perform overlap tests with a specified component, etc.

If you need to query the surroundings for overlapping/blocking geometry, you now have a suite of options to choose from.

11 – PREDICTING A PROJECTILE PATH

We have covered a large number of engine utilities designed to aid us when it comes to detecting collisions. We will wrap up this book with an example use of one of my favorite engine utilities—predicting a projectile path.

PredictProjectilePath

The Gameplay Statics static function library has a nice little gem that takes in parameters for a projectile and performs a number of single sphere traces along the predicted projectile's parabolic trajectory. The function produces an interesting collection of data, including the points along the projectile path itself, which can be used in all manner of creative ways.

The function can be configured to trace by collision channel or collision Object Type. It will return true if a hit is detected along the projectile path.

The function requires a world context object (as many static functions do), a Predict Projectile Path Params, and a Predict Projectile Path Result. An example setup would look like the following:

```
FPredictProjectilePathParams PathParams;
PathParams.LaunchVelocity = GetActorForwardVector()
* 600.f;
PathParams.bTraceWithChannel = true;
PathParams.bTraceWithCollision = true;
PathParams.TraceChannel = ECC_Visibility;
```

```
PathParams.ProjectileRadius = 5.f;
PathParams.ActorsToIgnore.Add(this);
PathParams.DrawDebugType =
EDrawDebugTrace::ForDuration;
PathParams.DrawDebugTime = 30.f;
PathParams.StartLocation = GetActorLocation() +
FVector(0.f, 0.f, 80.f);
PathParams.SimFrequency = 30.f;
PathParams.MaxSimTime = 1.f;
FPredictProjectilePathResult PathResult;
UGameplayStatics::PredictProjectilePath(this,
PathParams, PathResult);
```

In the above code snippet, we have set up the params to simulate a projectile with a velocity of 600. We chose to trace by channel, giving our trace the Visibility channel. We set bTraceWithCollision to true, enabling this function to detect blocking hits along the projectile path and stopping at the first blocking hit. Our sphere sweep radius is 5, and we have added the Character (this) to the Actors to ignore. We specified that we want a debug for a duration of 30 seconds (this will result in debug spheres along the projectile path). The starting location is at the Character's location plus 80 units up. The sim frequency is set to 30 (the higher this number, the more sub-steps in the projectile simulation). We set a maximum simulation time of 1 second (simulating a projectile flying for this long). The results are collected in the PathResult passed in by non-const reference.

The following shows the resulting debug spheres drawn for this trace.

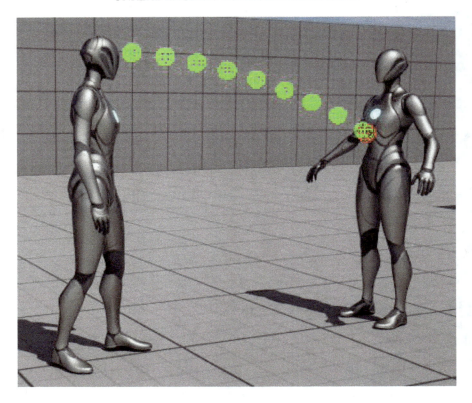

Figure 11.1 – Debug Spheres From Predicting a Projectile Path

The nice thing about `PredictProjectilePath` is that it accurately simulates the resulting projectile path you would get if you launched an actual projectile (in the engine) with the same starting location and velocity. This makes the function very useful even if you don't need collision (in which case you could simply set `bTraceWithCollision` to false and just simulate a projectile path).

You can retrieve the path points from the Predict Projectile Path Result struct as follows:

```
for (auto PathDatum : PathResult.PathData)
```

```
{
    DrawDebugSphere(
        GetWorld(),
        PathDatum.Location,
        15.f,
        24,
        FColor::White,
        false,
        30.f);
}
```

You can then use these path point locations in any way you wish, such as by creating a spline with points from this path. The following figure shows the debug spheres drawn with the above code snippet.

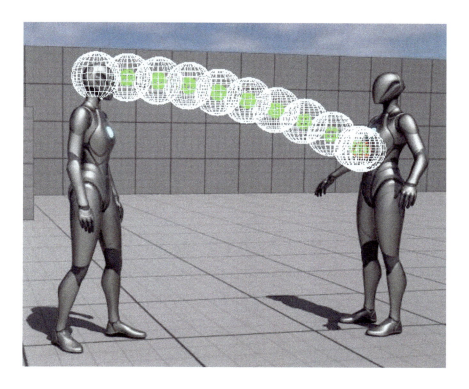

Figure 11.2 – Retrieving Path Data

Gameplay Statics exposes three functions to Blueprint for this utility.

Predict Projectile Path (Advanced)

This Blueprint-exposed function simply calls the native C++ function `PredictProjectilePath`. It takes in a Predict Projectile Path Params structure, and feeds that straight into the native C++ function.

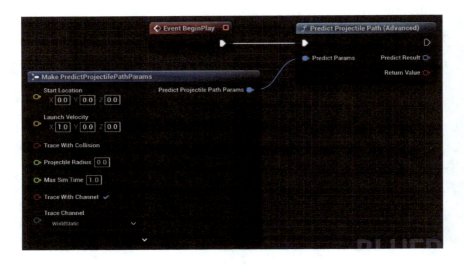

Figure 11.3 – Predict Projectile Path (Advanced)

Predict Projectile Path by TraceChannel

This is the Blueprint-exposed function with native C++ name `Blueprint_PredictProjectilePath_ByTraceChannel`. It takes in a collision trace channel among its other inputs and calls `PredictProjectilePath` under the hood. It traces by collision channel. The **Trace Path** input Boolean is used to set `bTraceWithCollision`, allowing you to choose whether the projectile path should trace for blocking hits.

Predict Projectile Path by ObjectType

This is the Blueprint-exposed function with native C++ name `Blueprint_PredictProjectilePath_ByObjectType`. It takes in a collision trace channel among its other inputs and calls `PredictProjectilePath` under the hood. It traces by collision Object Type. The **Trace Path** input Boolean is used to set `bTraceWithCollision`, allowing you to choose whether the projectile path should trace for blocking hits.

Tips

Keep these tips in mind when predicting projectile paths.

Disable tracing if you don't need to detect hits.

Set `bTraceWithCollision` to false (or **Trace Path** in Blueprints) if you don't need to detect hits. **Predict Projectile Path** performs sphere sweeps along the projectile path, and if you don't care about those sweep results (you only want to create the path) disabling tracing is a very important optimization.

Lower the Sim Frequency.

You may want a high simulation frequency for your projectile path. You don't need it. A value of 30 was chosen for the above example in C++ for demonstration purposes. Choose the lowest value that produces desirable results for you, as you should err on the side of performance rather than realism for video games.

12 – CONCLUSION

With great power comes great responsibility.

-Uncle Ben, to Peter Parker

Unreal Engine's collision framework is powerful. With that power comes responsibility. As we have seen, lots of things can be going on under the hood, unbeknownst to you and your development team. It may seem like the framework is overly complex and convoluted, but its features exist so that you can maximize the impact of your gameplay mechanics while minimizing the computational cost on the CPU.

Make use of collision filtering. It exists for a reason. While you're first starting out, learning the engine is your priority. At the learning stage, it's normal to create new components that overlap or block every single collision channel in the game. That's because you're just trying to get things working and figure out the basics of the system. But once you're past that point, it's time to start learning the proper way to configure your collision data.

One reason teams struggle with collision is because much of the collision data is generated by content creators. Collision profiles can be confusing for programmers, let alone artists and level designers. Because programmers make use of collision data while performing queries and scripting callbacks, it is important that the content creators producing that collision data are up to speed on the conventions of the project.

Teams would do well to have a document outlining the conventions for the creation and use of collision data. Important questions to ask are:

- Should just anyone be allowed to create new collision channels, or should channel creation be restricted?
- What do the collision channels mean for this project? Unreal Engine does not lay this out for you. Visibility, Pawn, WorldStatic, WorldDynamic, etc. are names that your project should specify uses for.
- Should there be a collision preset for all assets in the game? The use of Custom... for the Collision Presets on components presents a risk of introducing bugs to the project. Some teams disable the Custom... option entirely.
- Should an object ever be configured to Block or Overlap all? This should be a rare circumstance, rather than a default. Err on the side of Ignore for all channels *except the ones that the component needs to interact with.*

Communication is imperative. All members on a game development team need to be on the same page when it comes to collision. Without communication, there is chaos.

If your team has a well-defined set of conventions and everyone is on the same page, it makes for a more productive environment overall. Bugs are less likely, and when they do pop up, they're easier to track down. Gameplay mechanics are more performant. And overall, the team can feel more confident developing content and mechanics.

I hope this book has enlightened you on at least some aspects of the Unreal Engine collision framework and has provided you with a number of examples that you can refer back to when you need to implement a particular mechanic involving collision. Keep it on your shelf and crack it open occasionally to refresh on some of its concepts.

Thank you, dear reader, for your attention, your support, and for valuing the proper use of Unreal Engine's collision framework. May your game development dreams come to fruition with explosive success.

And as always, Happy Dev'ing.

Stephen

ABOUT THE AUTHOR

Stephen Ulibarri teaches game development full-time. He has over a decade of experience in Unreal Engine and C++, has developed surgical simulations for robotic surgery, and has taught over 400,000 students how to code and create video games. He runs the Druid Mechanics Discord Community, where he hosts progress meetings and fosters a positive environment for all learners who wish to pursue game development in all capacities.

www.ingramcontent.com/pod-product-compliance
Lightning Source LLC
La Vergne TN
LVHW051640050326
832903LV00022B/833